Bay Area Bouldering

Bay Area Bouldering

by Chris Summit

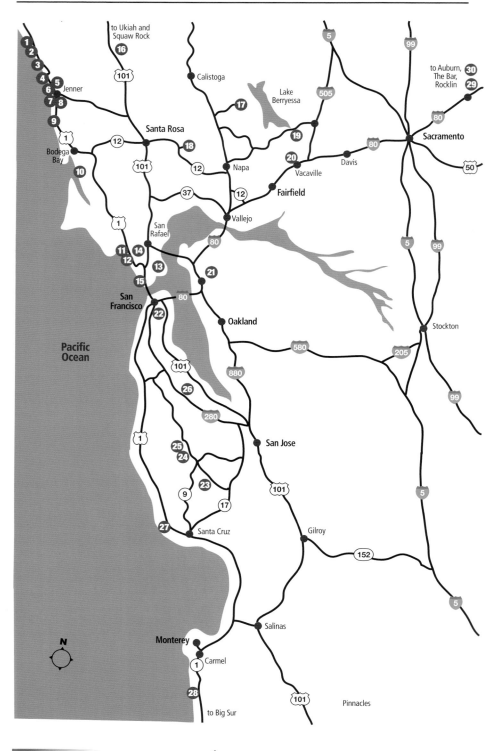

Contents

Warning.

Climbing is an inherently dangerous sport in which severe injuries or death may occur. Relying on the information in this book may increase the danger.

When climbing you can only rely on your skill, training, experience, and conditioning. **If you have any doubts as to your ability to safely climb any route in this guide, do not try it.**

This book is neither a professional climbing instructor nor a substitute for one. **It is not an instructional book. Do not use it as one.** It contains information that is nothing more than a compilation of opinions about bouldering in the Bay Area. **These opinions are neither facts nor promises.** Treat the information as opinions and nothing more. Do not substitute these opinions for your own common sense and experience.

Assumption of Risk

There may be errors in this book resulting from the mistake of the author and/or the people with whom they consulted. The information was gathered from a variety of sources, which may not have been independently verified. Those who provided the information may have made mistakes in their descriptions. The author may have made mistakes in their conveyance of the information in this book. **The author cannot, therefore, guarantee the correctness of any of the information contained in this book.** The topographical maps, photo-diagrams, difficulty ratings, protection ratings, approach and/or descent information, suggestions about equipment, and other matters may be incorrect or misleading. Fixed protection may be absent, unreliable, or misplaced. **You must keep in mind that the information in this book may be erroneous, so use your own judgement when choosing, approaching, climbing, or descending from a route described in this book.**

DO NOT USE THIS BOOK UNLESS YOU [AND YOUR ESTATE] PROMISE NEVER TO TRY TO SUE US IF YOU GET HURT OR KILLED.

Disclaimer of Warranties

THE AUTHOR AND PUBLISHER WARN THAT THIS BOOK CONTAINS ONLY THE AUTHOR'S OPINIONS ON THE SUBJECTS DISCUSSED. THEY MAKE NO OTHER WARRANTIES, EXPRESSED OR IMPLIED, OF MERCHANTABILITY, FITNESS FOR PURPOSE, OR OTHERWISE, AND IN ANY EVENT, THEIR LIABILITY FOR BREACH OF ANY WARRANTY OR CONTRACT WITH RESPECT TO THE CONTENT OF THIS BOOK IS LIMITED TO THE PURCHASE PRICE OF THE BOOK. THEY FURTHER LIMIT TO SUCH PURCHASE PRICE THEIR LIABILITY ON ACCOUNT OF ANY KIND OF NEGLIGENT BEHAVIOR WHATSOEVER ON THEIR PART WITH RESPECT TO THE CONTENTS OF THIS BOOK.

Acknowledgements

Thank you local boulderers for your first ascents:

Russ Bobzien, Scott Frye, Chris Sharma, Greg Loh, Scott Cosgrove, John Sherman, Barry Bates, John "Yabo" Yablonski, Dave Caunt, Bruce Morris, Mike Papciak, Nat Smale, Ken Ariza, Tom Richardson, Harrison Dekker, Jim Thornburg, Mark Howe, Marcos Nunez, Richie Esquibel, Charlie Barrett, Sean Brady, Ryan Tolentino, Jerry Dodrill, Kevin Jorgeson, Shawn Rogers, Frankie Ocasio and Aaron Rough.

Thanks to these people for their help with the guide:

My wonderful mom Jeanie Anderson-Saludes and awesome step-dad Bony Saludes, my beautiful girlfriend Valentine Cullen and her incredible daughter Holly Anne (inspiration), Chris McNamara (obviously), Bruce Morris, Scott Frye, Jim Thornburg, John Sherman, Russ Bobzien, Richie Esquibel, Charlie Barrett, Sean Brady, Ken Ariza, Marcos Nunez and Dave Buchanan.

Book Credits

*2nd print - 2010
Written by Chris Summit
Photos by Chris Summit (unless otherwise noted)
Edited by Steve McNamara, Chris McNamara
Layout by Chris McNamara

Cover Photo: Valentine Cullen at Turtle Rock. *Photo by Jerry Dodrill*
Back Cover Photo: Chris Summit on the Hard Traverse, Goat Rock. *Photo by Jerry Dodrill*
Contents photo: Bay Area Sunset *Photo by Valentine Cullen*
Cover Design *by* David Safanda Design Solutions.
www.safanda.com

Printed in China

Introduction

By Chris Summit

The rock of the Bay Area is as diverse as the landscape and people who live here. Sandstone, schist, rhyolite, basalt, and chert are the most prevalent types of stone found locally and they each offer a unique experience. A few crags with sport and trad climbing can be found around the Bay, but the abundance of rock is just the right size for bouldering. All along the breathtaking Pacific Coast, from the Mendocino County line south past the Golden Gate to Big Sur, is a rich variety of stone to choose from in an incredibly scenic environment. Inland hills, mountains, rivers, and lakes also have great bouldering in lush forests and on golden, grassy hillsides. Most boulders are close by cities and highways and on the many fine beaches and offer an almost endless supply of easily accessible problems. As I am sure you will find in this guide, great bouldering is never too far away from wherever you are around the Bay.

SuperTopo.com

All the Bay Area info below is available at www.supertopo.com with links directly to the sources for easier trip planning.

When to climb

You can boulder year round at all areas in this book. That said, each area has its own sweet time to visit. The Bay Area is full of many microclimates and the weather at each area changes drastically throughout the year and often throughout the day. It can be 50 degrees cold and foggy at Stinson Beach and at the same moment 100 degrees hot and muggy at Vacaville.

Short of a massive winter storm, there is usually always some place in the Bay Area with good bouldering conditions. I have done my best to provide an overview of the weather for each specific area but it will still take some time to understand the ever-changing conditions and be able to plan your bouldering accordingly.

North Coast Camping

Jenner/Fort Ross

Just a couple miles north of the Fort Ross bouldering area and about 16 miles north of Jenner on CA-1 is Stillwater Cove Campground. call (707) 847-3245. A few miles north of Fort Ross and Stillwater Cove and about 20 miles north of Jenner on CA-1 is the amazing Salt Point State Park and the radical Salt Point bouldering areas. Camping is available at Gerstle Cove Campground and Woodside Campground. Call (707) 847-3221. or 1 800 444 PARK.

Jenner/Bridgehaven

Pomo Canyon Campground is off CA-1 just south of Jenner and CA-116 and just north of Goat Rock State Park in Bridgehaven. Take Willow Creek Rd. east from CA-1 for about 2.5 miles to the right turn onto the dirt road that leads to the campground. CLOSED IN WINTER.

Jenner/Guerneville

Austin Creek State Recreation Area in Guerneville is adjacent to the awe-inspiring Armstrong Redwoods State Reserve. The majestic grove of giant primeval redwood trees is a glimpse of how the whole area used to look before logging. Camping is available at Bullfrog Pond for $15 per night. Call (707) 869-2015. Between Jenner and Guerneville on Moscow Rd. off of River Rd. (CA-116) in Duncan's Mills is the popular riverside campground, Casini Ranch. Call (800) 451-8400.

Kevin Jorgeson on the Hard Arête (V2), Goat Rock State Park.
Photo by Jerry Dodrill www.jerrydodrill.com.

North Coast Dining and Amenities

The nearest climbing gear retailers for the North Coast are Sonoma Outfitters and REI in Santa Rosa, an hour drive inland (east).

Jenner

A gas station/mini mart/deli is the main stop in Jenner. The excellent River's End restaurant offers fine food, wine, and sunsets. The Sizzling Tandoor on the corner of CA-1 and Willow Creek Rd. (the road to Pomo Canyon Campground and bouldering area) just south of Jenner also has great food and views.

Bodega Bay

Less than ten miles south of the Jenner climbing areas is the quiet fishing village and beach getaway of Bodega Bay. Get gas at the Texaco on CA-1 and food, beer, and supplies at Diekman's Store, also on CA-1. Enjoy the catch of the day with great views of the bay at The Tides Wharf and Restaurant (seen in Alfred Hitchcock's classic The Birds).

Guerneville

More than you may ever need can be found in Guerneville about 12 miles east of Jenner. From Jenner (CA-1) take River Rd. (CA-116) east for about 12 miles to Guerneville and gas, a 24hr Safeway, the mui delicioso taco wagon usually in the Safeway parking lot and the scrumptious Andorno's Pizza (16205 1st St.).

North Bay Camping

Marin County

Marin has camping available at Mount Tamalpais State Park (near the Mount Tamalpais bouldering areas), Samuel P. Taylor State Park (15 minutes west of US-101 on Sir Francis Drake Blvd.) and Point Reyes National Seashore. For reservations at Mount Tamalpais or Samuel P. Taylor contact Reserve America or for information about camping at Point Reyes call (415) 663-8054.

Napa/Lake Berryessa

Lake Berryessa has seven private resorts that have camping. Most of the resorts are on the west and south shores off CA-128 or Knoxville Rd. only a few miles from the Vacaville and Putah Creek bouldering areas. Napa has a good campground: Skyline Wilderness Park on 2201 Imola Ave., which is about 15 miles west of Lake Berryessa and the Putah Creek bouldering area. Call (707) 252-0481.

Santa Rosa/Kenwood

Sugarloaf Ridge State Park off CA-12 just west of Kenwood and east of US-101 in Santa Rosa has good boulders within walking distance of the campground. Take Adobe Canyon Rd. from CA-12 for a few miles to the park entrance and campground. Call (800) 444-PARK.

North Bay Dining and Amenities

Marin County

Brooklyn Pizza at 900 Andersen Dr. and High Tech Burrito at 484 Las Gallinas or 2042 4th St., San Rafael. Just off US-101 in Corte Madera (south of San Rafael) is an REI with almost everything you'll need for climbing or camping. Take the same Paradise Dr./Tamalpais Dr. exit as for the Ring Mountain bouldering area, but go to the shopping center on the west side of US-101 off Tamalpais Dr. A couple miles west of 101 on Tamalpais Dr. is downtown Larkspur and the historic Lark Creek Inn at 234 Magnolia Ave. Partake in the happy hour (M-F half off beer and cocktails) and enjoy delicious, seasonal, farm fresh cuisine. The Oceanside town of Stinson Beach (near Stinson and Mickey's Beach bouldering areas) has a good market: Beckers by the Beach has good food, drink, and supplies. Other fine dining in town can be found at the summertime snack bar adjacent to the beach that has good hot dogs and soda or for a bit more fancy try the Sand Dollar on CA-1.

Napa/Sonoma

An assortment of gas stations, stores and restaurants can be found off CA-12 and CA-29 in downtown Napa or Sonoma. In Napa try the muy bueno High Tech Burrito 641 Trancas St. (off CA-29). In Sonoma enjoy a Bay Area original, the delicious Mary's Pizza Shack in the Sonoma Plaza and on Sonoma Hwy. (CA-12).

Santa Rosa/Kenwood

Santa Rosa is one hour north of San Francisco on US-101 and has all the amenities you might need: gas, climbing/camping gear (Sonoma Outfitters, REI and Vertex) and indoor climbing at Vertex. A wide variety of dining is available in Santa Rosa. Try the Russian River Brewing Company on Fourth St. in downtown or the tasty Taqueria Santa Rosa or China Room in Rincon Valley. Or just east of Santa Rosa in quiet little Kenwood try the Mexican/Spanish cuisine at the Vineyards Inn on the corner of Sonoma Hwy (CA-12) and Adobe Canyon Rd. (the road to Sugarloaf Ridge State Park bouldering area and campground).

East Bay Camping

Oakland/Berkeley

Southeast of Oakland and Berkeley camping is available at Lake Chabot in Anthony Chabot Regional Park. From I-580 east in Castro Valley take the Redwood Rd. exit and turn left onto Redwood Rd. or from I-580 west take the Castro Valley exit and turn left onto Castro Valley Blvd., then right onto Redwood Rd and follow it to the park. Call in advance (510) 562-2267.

Oakland/San Jose

Camping is available in the hills between Oakland and San Jose at Sunol Regional Wilderness near Pleasanton. Take I-580 east to I-680 south to Calaveras Rd/CA-84, turn left onto Calaveras, then take Geary Rd. to the park. Enjoy a short hike and some fine basalt cragging at Indian Joe Caves on Indian Joe Creek Trail inside the park. Call in advance (510) 562-2267

Vacaville/Lake Berryessa

Lake Berryessa has seven private resorts that have camping. Most of the resorts are on the west and south shores off CA-128 or Knoxville Rd. only a few miles from the Putah Creek and Vacaville bouldering areas.

East Bay Dining and Amenities

Oakland/Emeryville
Try the eclectic mix of food vendors at the Emeryville Public Market (5959 Shellmound St.). It's off I-80/I-580/I-880 in Emeryville south of Berkeley and north of Oakland. Take the Powell St. exit east to Shellmound St.

Berkeley
Gas, food, climbing/camping gear (REI and Marmot), and the largest indoor climbing gym in the Bay Area: Berkeley Ironworks. Enjoy an eccentric assortment of food and shops on the busy Telegraph Ave. in downtown Bezerkly (take Ashby Ave. a few miles east of I-80).

Vacaville
Gas, food and shopping malls right off I-80 only a few miles from the Vacaville Open Space bouldering areas.

South Bay Camping

Big Basin
Big Basin Redwoods State Park (the first State Park in California) – 25 miles north of Santa Cruz and about 65 miles south of San Francisco on CA-236 near the town of Boulder Creek and just a short drive from the Castle Rock, Aquarian Valley and Skyline bouldering areas. Call (800) 444-PARK

San Jose/Castle Rock
Camping is available at Castle Rock State Park about a three mile hike from the parking lot. The primitive sites are about $10 per night and are first come, first serve. Near the city of Saratoga on Big Basin Way is a nice campground called Saratoga Springs with RV and tent camping.

Monterey/Big Sur
South of Monterey, Carmel, the Granite Creek bouldering area and the Bay Area, the bold and beautiful Big Sur has an abundance of camping available in State Parks, National Forest, and private resorts. Try Pfeiffer Big Sur State Park. Call (837) 667-2315

South Bay Dining and Amenities

San Francisco
Pier 39 and Fisherman's Wharf have good food and fun. San Francisco's Chinatown is one of the largest outside of Asia and offers fine food all day and all night. Mission Cliffs has indoor climbing and gear in a good atmosphere. For gear go to The North Face at 180 Post St. Get gas and food on either CA-1 or US-101.

San Jose/Santa Cruz
For great beer and food at reasonable prices enjoy Gordon Biersch Brewing Company on 33 E. San Fernando St. (downtown San Jose). A gas station/mini mart/deli and popular motorcycle hangout is at the intersection of CA-35 (Skyline Blvd.) and CA-84 in Sky Londa a few miles north of the Aquarian Valley and Skyline bouldering areas and across the street from the infamous Alice's Restaurant (where you can get what you want). Pacific Edge is a great indoor climbing gym and gear retailer in Santa Cruz (104 Bronson St.). If you feel like having more fun in the sun then don't miss the oldest amusement park in California: the Santa Cruz Beach Boardwalk.

Monterey
Gas, food, supplies, climbing gear and indoor climbing (Sanctuary Rock Gym in Sand City) are all located just a few miles apart near CA-1. Don't miss the restaurants on the famous Cannery Row and the Monterey Bay Aquarium.

Bouldering Ratings Compared

Hueco	Y.D.S	Font
VB	5.0-5.8	<3
V0-	5.9	3/4-
V0	5.10a/b	4-/4/4+
V0+	5.10c/d	4+
V1	5.11a/b	4+/5-
V2	5.11b/c	5/5+
V3	5.11c/d	6a/b
V4	5.12a/b	6c/c+
V5	5.12b/c	7a
V6	5.12c/d	7a+
V7	5.13a/b	7a+/7b
V8	5.13b/c	7b/7b+
V9	5.13c/d	7b+/7c
V10	5.14a	7c/7c+
V11	5.14b	7c+/8a
V12	5.14c	8a+
V13	5.14d	8b
V14	5.14d/5.15a	8b+
V15	5.15a/b	8c
V16	5.15b/c	8c+

History

By Chris Summit

Bouldering in the Bay Area started as far back as the 1920s on the volcanic rhyolite crags at Indian Rock Park in Berkeley. Some of the original rock climbing pioneers of Yosemite and America, Dick Leonard, "the father of modern rock climbing," and David Brower learned and practiced rock climbing and the first dynamic belays at Indian Rock. They used ropes mainly, but scrambling and bouldering were also practiced. The first modern day bouldering in the Bay Area also took place at Indian Rock and its partner in climb Mortar Rock up the road in the late 1960s and early 1970s. A few young soon-to-be rock stars, John "The Verm" Sherman (inventor of the V-scale for rating difficulty) and Scott Frye (first ascents of some of the best sport climbs of the west), and an unknown (except in Berkeley) rock climbing star named Nat Smale (popular for putting up Nat's Traverse at Mortar Rock in 1976, which for a short time was the hardest boulder traverse in the country) and a few other characters all sent the problems and greased the holds long before the rest of the country even heard of bouldering.

The late 70s and early 80s were the heydays for first ascents around the Bay Area as bouldering grew in popularity. While Berkeley's volcanic boulders were getting developed, across the Bay a young Marin County climber named Russ Bobzien was busy establishing the original North Bay classics on the schist of Ring Mountain, Stinson Beach and Mickey's Beach. The awesome Parking Lot Boulder at Castle Rock (the sandstone boulder forest reminiscent of France's famous Fontainebleau) was also getting developed at that time by more of California' soon-to-be rock stars like J-Tree stone master Scott Cosgrove, John

"Yabo" Yablonski, Barry Bates, and even the Yosemite stone master, Ron Kauk. I guess sport climbing took over for most of the later 80s because I can't remember much bouldering development going on after the early part. (Hold on, I can't remember much of the eighties at all.) I think cleaning new problems would have got our fancy tights dirty and besides, with a new wave of bolted sport climbs all over the country back then, why pebble wrestle? Silly tights wearing kooks (myself included), we could have scored many great first ascents around the Bay Area that would sit untouched until another wave of bouldering madness took over in the 1990s.

The creation of the crash pad in the 1990s more than doubled the potential bouldering that could be done and reignited the bouldering flame. The Bay Area, along with all the other bouldering areas in the world, were changed forever. New boulder problems were found and put up right next to old school classics and sit starts were added to everything. One of the best problems in the Bay Area was put up in the late 1990s, an old Yabo project at Castle Rock climbed by the local and now world famous Chris Sharma, called Eco Terrorist V10. Berkeley has also seen a constant flow of new problems, along with talented boulderers to send them. Greg Loh, Randy Puro, Mike Papciak, Mark Nicholas, and the relentless Scott Frye have all added test-pieces of their own over the last decade, culminating with Frye's newest classics on Grizzly Peak and Sharma's 2004 ascent of The Impossible Traverse V13 at Mortar Rock (the hardest problem in the Bay Area, so far). The future project at Mortar would be to do the complete traverse starting on Nat's Traverse (V8), then reversing the crux moves on Marks Traverse (V11) into The Impossible Traverse to finish. To the east The Vacaville Boulders got a lot of new problems in the late 90s and into the 21st century courtesy of the Bezerkly Crew, local Aaron Rough, and also my buddies and I. At Mickey's Beach Kenny Ariza established some new problems on the South Side Boulders and the strong, talented Frankie Ocasio has also been busy doing new, hard problems right up to press time. The boulders that got the most development in the last decade and are still being developed are on the North Coast. Locals and friends Marcos Nunez, Richie "The Pirate" Esquibel, Jim and Jason Campbell, Sean Brady, Charlie Barrett, Ryan Tolentino, Kevin Jorgeson, Mark Howe, Jordi Morgan, and I have done hundreds of first ascents from V0–Vhard on the schist, chert and sandstone crags on and around Sonoma County's one-of-a-kind coastline.

The present and the future look good for the Bay Area bouldering scene. New problems are still being found at old areas and new areas are still being found and developed. While making this guide I had to stop the press several times because someone showed me new problems. The first time I had to stop the press was when local climber/photographer extraordinaire Jerry Dodrill showed me some new problems he found at Marshall Gulch, a place I had climbed for the first time as a child. My mom said the other kids would run out to play in the water, but I would go the opposite direction and climb up the cliffs and boulders.

The next stop the press came when my good friend and local boulderer Ken Ariza told me about the obvious classics on the boulders on Dillon Beach. An area I had driven by hundreds of times—doh!

The final stop the press was one day when I was inspired by the view of Mount Tamalpais from Mac's home in Mill Valley while working on the guidebook. I decided to avoid the 101 rush hour and take the much longer route home over Mt. Tam and up the coast to look for new boulders. I parked at the first area I saw potential on Mt Tam and I charged off into the forest. After checking out a few small obvious chunks with some barely worthy problems

Russ Bobzien on Manitou (V11). Photo Russ Bobzien Collection.

I was about to call it quits and hit the road to another zone when my intuition pulled me over one more hill right to a couple big virgin boulders and one of the best lines on the mountain I called "Intuition" (V5).

History has many lessons to teach us, two of the most important i feel are simply to enjoy yourself and to make the most out of what you've got. Get out there and hike around your neck of the woods and look in those unexplored areas where you think new boulders might be hiding. They're out there waiting to be found and climbed. We don't need to travel all the time or climb in the gym all the time. Incredibly diverse, world class bouldering is right in our own backyard.

Salt Point

Number of problems: **100+**

Rock: **Sandstone**

Difficulty: **VB-V9, mostly V0-V7**

Tafoni sandstone cliffs and boulders abound in this marvelous natural playground. Some of the original streets of San Francisco are paved with stone from this park that was brought down the coast by boat. All of the bouldering in the park is a bit far from the Bay Area but it is all totally worth the drive. Sport and traditional climbing, hiking, diving, mushroom picking, whale watching, fishing, surfing, and oh-yes, bouldering can all be enjoyed in the park year round. Peace and solitude can also be found on the many secret beaches and forgotten boulders. There are hundreds of established boulder problems on the unique sandstone, starting from 3rd and 4th class scrambles up huge spires to radical V0-V9 problems on gritty slopers and amazing pocketed tafoni.

Marcos Nunez gets high over the surf.

Shroomland/Waterfall Boulders

Shroom Boulder Classics: **Vise Grip V4** (east face of the Shroom Boulder).
Waterfall Boulders Classics: **Waterfall Crack V3r, High Times V0x** (face/crack).
Diamond Boulder Classics: **Diamond in the Rough V3** (right face), **Matrix V5** (center), **Left Eye V7** (left arête).
Directions: Park on the east side of CA-1 in a small turnout next to the Shroom Boulder 22.0 mi. north of the CA-116/CA-1 intersection and 6.0 miles south of Skaggs Springs Rd. The Waterfall Boulders are across CA-1 to the west and along the beach south of the tranquil waterfall. The gem of the area, The Diamond Boulder, is the furthest south.

Johnny Cash Boulders

Classics: **Yellowfoot V3, Johnny Cash V5.**
Directions: For North Shroomland, park on the west side of CA-1 in a small turnout next to an old picket fence just north of the parking for South Shroomland. Hike across the highway into the forest toward a big rock. The Johnny Cash Boulders are up and left of Big Rock and the turnout and The Hourglass Boulder is up and right. Big Rock is visible from CA-1 and has a few good V0-3 problems.

Fisk Mill Cove Boulders

Classics: **Off The Heezey V1r, Jugular V1r** (lower cliff). **Fisk Mill Traverse V3** (upper cliff). *Directions:* 22.7 miles north of the CA-116/CA-1 intersection and about 5.3 miles south of Skaggs Springs Rd. off CA-1. Just north of the parking for Shroomland is the left turn into the parking lot of Fisk Mill Cove. Park in either the south or the first north parking area. The boulder problems are on the rocky hill visible from the road between the north and south parking areas. The far north parking area accesses more boulder problems and sport climbs around Sentinel Rock.

Fort Ross

Number of problems: 25

Rock: Sandstone

Difficulty: VB-V11, mostly V1-V6

The Fort Ross Boulders were discovered by the visionary local climber Richie Esquibel in the summer of 1996. His discovery helped usher in a new era of bouldering on the sandstone of the North Coast. Richie, along with Marcos Nunez, developed the original classics on the main overhanging face of the Fort Ross Boulder. These are some of the best and most challenging problems on the entire Pacific Coast. The steep problems on the main face start low and top out high, with big moves between blocky edges and sandpaper slopes. Most of the year they have soft sandy landings that allow for fearless dynos and carefree falls.

Richie Esquibel "Living a Dream" (V6).

About the rock

Mostly solid and steep, overhanging sedimentary and conglomerate sandstone. The main face of the main boulder is about 12 to 15 feet high in summer and about 15 to 20 feet high in winter when the sand is low. The rest of the boulders are mostly smaller with rocky landings and require a low tide.

When to climb

Good conditions all year except for mid-winter. Sand levels change throughout the year—in the middle of winter the sandy landing under the main boulder drops down to its lowest point exposing ankle breaking rocks. Big waves crash onto the beach and deposit driftwood and seaweed, making the landings even a bit nastier still. During this time the boulder problems are almost

R-rated solos. This three-four month period fluctuates between the months of November and March and is the only time when conditions are unpredictable. In summer the sand is usually at its highest and can make the problems feel almost too low. Sometimes the higher sand level can also make a few of the classic sit starts un-climbable for a few months unless you do a little digging for footholds. The rest of the year it's usually perfect, with soft sandy landings and good dry conditions. With the minor exception of foggy days just after a rain when this north-east facing boulder gets no sun and may take up to a whole extra day or two to dry compared to other rocks on the coast.

Driving directions

From the Bay Area, take US-101 north to Petaluma, exit East Washington St. and

Number of problems by difficulty

VB	V0	V1	V2	V3	V4	V5	V6	V7	V8	V9	V10	≥V11
2	6	5	4	12	6	5	2	3	2	1	1	0

follow it west through town. Washington St. turns into Bodega Ave. and then to Valley Ford Rd. before connecting with CA-1. Go north on CA-1 about 18 miles (about nine miles north of Bodega Bay) to the CA-116 (River Rd.)/CA-1 intersection just south of Jenner.

From Santa Rosa area, on US-101 exit Mark West Springs Rd./River Rd. Head west on River Rd. for about 15 miles to Guerneville and the CA-116 intersection. Continue west on River Rd./CA-116 for about 12 miles toward CA-1 and Jenner. Just before (south of) Jenner you'll come to the CA-1 intersection.

From the CA-116 (River Rd.)/CA1 intersection just south of Jenner turn right (north) onto CA-1. Set your odometer and drive for 14.0 miles (thru the town of

Jenner) to the parking in pullouts on the left (west) side of CA-1.

Coming from north of Jenner (Mendocino) on CA-1 set your odometer at Skaggs Springs Rd./CA-1 intersection (south of Annapolis and Gualala) and drive south on CA-1 for 14.0 miles to the parking in a pullout on the right (west) side of CA-1 about 1 mile north of Fort Ross State Historic Park. Parking lot GPS 38.5235, -123.263317

Approach

Fort Ross Boulders are on the beach also known as Kolmers Gulch about a hundred feet below the highway. A short (two-minute) steep downhill hike from the car will get you to the beach and the boulders.

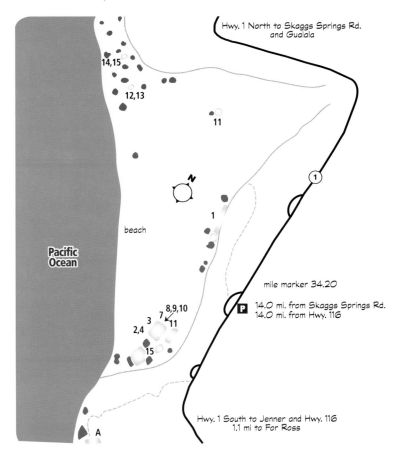

Traverse Cliff

❏ **1. The Fort Ross Traverse V1★★★** Stand start on the far right or far left side of cliff face and traverse, using all holds from side to side. V2 Low.

Main Boulders

GPS: 38.523167, -123.263817

❏ **2. Swiss Cheese V0★★** Stand start on swiss cheese pockets and go up right arête.

❏ **3. Swiss Cheese Traverse V1★★** Same stand start as #2 but traverse up and left, past sloper into highball slab face.

❏ **4. Irie Traverse V8★★** Stand start same as #2 and #3, then traverse left same as #3 to slab. Catch a rest, then turn the corner and pass #7. Continue traversing left to the jug on #9 and drop down a few moves to the ball on the sit start of #9 and then do the sit start of #11 to finish. V7 if you start on #7.

❏ **5. Living La Vida Loca V8★★★★** Sit start on right hand edge and left hand sloper gaston, then wrestle your way up past sloper meat-wraps on mini arête into #7. FA: Chris Summit.

❏ **6. Grand Finale V9★★★★** Sit start on sloper pinch, then up into #5 to finish. Or: Low sand, lower edge sigt start V9/10! FA: Ryan Tolentino.

❏ **6a. Relentless V10★★** Do V9 #6 sit start into #4 to finish. Or: Low sand, lower edge sit start V10/11!! FA: Ryan Tolentino.

❏ **7. Living a Dream V6★★★★** Stand start on right hand side-pull and left hand under-cling. Ascend highball face left of arête. Row gently downstream for life is but a dream. FA: Marcos Nunez/Richie Esquibel.

❏ **8. The Shazinky V8★★★** Sit start on the loose ball-shaped hold, then angle up and right staying below the jug/ledge on #9 and #10 up into #7 to finish. FA: Richie Esquibel.

❏ **9. Fort Rossta V6★★★★** Same sit start as #8 on the ball, then straight up past under-cling side-pulls to jug. Throw a big move to gain the rails below the lip and top out. **V4 Variation:** Stand start on under-cling side-pulls, to jug, to top. FA: Marcos Nunez.

❏ **9a. Flying Monkey V7★★★** Stand start same as #9, then dyno/lunge/fly from the jug/shelf in the center of the face all the way to the sloper rail below the top. V8 sit start. FA: Charlie Barrett

❏ **10. Living a Nightmare V7★★★** Same sit start on the ball as #8 and #9 and same first crux as #9 to jug, then traverse the sloper ledge to the right up into #7 to finish. FA: Chris Summit

❏ **11. Left Arête V6★★★** Same sit start as #8, #9 and #10 on the loose ball, then diagonal traverse up and left into the left arête. V5 if you stand start from the jug rail.

❏ **12. Left Hook V7★★** Same sit start as #11 on ball, then traverse to far left to top of #13. It's a V6 if you stand start from jug rail.

❏ **13. V1★** Stand start slopey, sandy mantel.

❏ **14. V6★** Low start roof on backside. V1 stand start.

❏ **15. Scrunch and Munch V2★★** Sit start on a big horizontal rail at the base of a short arête boulder with a rocky landing behind the main boulder. Climb the arête to a scrunchy, slopey mantle finish.

North Cove

The boulders in the North Cove are much less traveled and therefore have much sandier rock. A quick brushing will take care of the sand. The rock can also be more brittle, so be careful. Be careful not only for your own safety (duh) but also be careful not to break the precious holds off the boulders. Take extra caution not to climb the rocks in the North Cove or any of the sandstone at Fort Ross, or anywhere else on the North Coast for that matter, when it is damp because it will be even more brittle than it already is. Most of the boulders in the North Cove have rocky landings. Pads are good.

❑ **16. The Creek Boulder** V0★ Climb the north or south face.

❑ **17. Octopussy** V2★★ Sit start on sloper ledge and traverse right along ledge to topout.

❑ **18. Orca** V0★★ Sit start on detached block or stand start in hueco to rail to top.

❑ **19. Albatross** V4★★ Sit start on right hand lie-back—go up past pockets to topout up and right on top of #18. V2 if you stand start at pockets.

❑ **20. Apocalyptic Bebop** V4★★ Same sit start as #19 and pocket crux, then top out up left. V2 if you stand start at pockets.

Jerry Dodrill takes a cruise on You Snooze You Loose, (V3).

South Cove (AKA The Tide-line Boulders)

Local climbing angler Marcos Nunez discovered the Tide-line c.2000.
He had the place to himself until 2005 when a few psyched locals re-discovered it and gave it the nickname The Tide-line Boulders. Most boulders have rocky landings, so bring many pads.

❏ **21. Tide-line Traverse V4★★** Sit or stand start on tafoni jugs on the far right side of the rightmost of the two main boulders. Traverse left across the face, then bridge the gap from one boulder to the other and continue traversing left into #27 to finish.

❏ **22. V0★★** Sandy prow.

❏ **23. Smearnoff V4★★** Sit or stand start same as the Tide-line Traverse (#21) but only traverse across the face of the first boulder, then drop down into #25 to finish.

❏ **24. V1★★** Sit start on right hand lie-back crack pinch and left hand pocket, then go up the short juggy lie-back crack to the slopey topout.

❏ **25. Borscht V3★★** Same sit start as #24 on right hand lie-back crack pinch and left hand pocket, then make a few moves up and left past a small pocket/slot and up out of the mini cave.

❏ **26. Been There Done That V2★★★** Sit start on the right side of the leftmost of the two main boulders on large bulbous knobby features and go up and left to tafoni topout.

❏ **27. You Snooze You Loose V3★★** Sit start just down and left of the bulbous knobs start of #26 on a left hand scoop and a right hand pinch and go up and left to the arête or top out straight up.

❏ **28. Mangel Wurzel V5★★** Sit start below #27 finish on the base of the left arête (#29), then traverse right past #26 into #25 to finish. **V4Variation:** Traverse past #22 to far right.

❏ **29. V0★★** Sit start left arête same as #28.

❏ **30. ??**

Sea Crag

Number of problems: **20-30 problems**

Rock: **Schist/Chert**

Difficulty: **VB-V6**

Some of the most difficult sport climbs in the Bay Area are on the main face of the Sea Crag and some of the most far out bouldering can be found there as well. The schist boulders that surround Sea Crag have problems from 5.0-V6 with mostly rocky or watery landings. Pads, spotters, and cajones will help, but good old fashioned skills will work the best. The massive chert boulder in the north cove known as The Humpback with its beach front property and highball problems over sandy landings is the main attraction by far. The striations in the chert offer in-cut horizontal fingertip edges a lot like the rock at the popular Glen Canyon in San Francisco. It is found on the beach in the cove to the north of the Sea Crag. Classics adorn every side of this huge "whale" of a boulder with overhanging problems on the eastside and vertical-slabby highballs on all the rest. Sandy landings mixed with rocks at different times of year require pads and a low tide is also best for The Humpback unless you don't mind getting your shoes wet.

Classics: **Humpback V6** (southeast face), **Medula-Oblongota V5** (humpback into Hibi Gibis), **Chalka Khan V4** (southeast arête), **Hibi Gibis V3** (east face, left), and **South Face V0R** (easy way up/down) all on the amazing southeast face of The Humpback Boulder.

Richie Esquibel (on the now extinct) Humpback (V6). Photo by Jamal Hemenway.

Driving Directions/Approach

6.2 miles north of CA-116/CA-1 intersection and 21.8 miles south of Skaggs Springs Rd. on CA-1 north of Jenner. Turn off the highway into the parking lot for the Sonoma Coast State Beach Vista Trail. Follow a small trail downhill (west) past the bathroom, then down and right over an old fence. Then go a short ways to a rocky outcropping before heading left down the steep hill along the ridgeline. Head for the saddle on the top of the huge egg-shaped Sea Crag. Be careful on the final descent into the saddle. Scramble up over the back of the Sea Crag to most of the problems or from the saddle hike north downhill to the Humpback Boulder in the North Cove.

Twin Coves

Number of problems: **10-20 problems**

Rock: **Schist/Graywacke Sandstone**

Difficulty: **VB-V4**

Mark Howe on his classic Solo Arête 5.6X.
Photo by Jerry Dodrill

North of Jenner, off the side of the beautiful Pacific Coast Hwy. is a large cove split in two by an island of schist spires. The island of rock is actually connected to the mainland by a narrow isthmus that is almost completely submerged in the ocean at high tide. Seals, birds and fish swim, fly, and float by in a constant show of mother nature's glory. A good low tide boulder can be found in the south cove and a few problems with rocky landings can be found among the crags on the island but the best is the Isthmus Boulder, which is on the south side of the isthmus. Some of the rock is loose; a pad and spotter is highly recommended. The boulder problems at Twin Coves vary in difficulty from 5.6-V4. There are also good sport climbs on the "island" ranging from 5.6-5.10.

Classics: **Solo Arête 5.6X** (down climb), **Twin Coves Traverse V3** (base of solo arête), and the **Isthmus Boulder V0-V3.**

Driving Directions/Approach

3.1 miles north of the CA-116/CA-1 intersection on CA-1 (The Pacific Coast Highway) and 24.9 miles south of Skaggs Springs Rd. north of Jenner, park in the turnouts on the west side of CA-1 (mile marker 23.31). Hike down a steep trail to the south cove, then walk north to the isthmus that divides the cove in two to access the island of rock.

Usually only in winter will high tides cover the isthmus and that is rare. Parking in the larger turnout about 1/4 mile north of the south cove parking (mile marker 23.65) is about the same. Hike the trail downhill to the north cove and walk south along the beach to the obvious island of spires.

Super Slab

Number of problems: 25

Rock: Blue Schist

Difficulty: VB-V9, mostly V0-V7

Super Slab, originally called Not So Super Slab by the old school Sonoma County rock climbing pioneer Mark Howe, is a roadside attraction that should not be missed. Back when Mark found the place in the 1980s, rock climbing was still new to the Sonoma Coast. That's probably why he only did the obvious 5.6 slabs and then went on to the bigger rocks up north. For years he told a couple of buddies and myself about it but we never bothered checking it out. One fine day my old friend Shawn Rogers and I were on our way home from our first trip to the newly-discovered Fort Ross Boulders. We both thought, "Damn, if that sandstone up on the North Coast (that we used to think was too crumbly) is actually that good, then maybe we should check out this 'Not So Super Slab' place on our way home. What if it's actually super?" So we pulled off the highway into the big turnout right below the crag and bushwhacked our way up toward the small outcrop. We were psyched to find just what we were looking for: hidden behind layers of thick shrubbery were some great looking boulder problems. After a little landscaping to clear out the base of the boulder and to make a good trail, we soon had about five to ten new classics. It wouldn't take long before we had dropped the "Not So" from the old name and started respectfully calling the place Super Slab.

Liz Larson climbs The Virgin (V0).

When to climb

Any time of year can offer good conditions, but as with most of the North Coast areas, the mid-winter months are generally wetter and colder. Summer can be a bit warm to pull on the sloper handholds of the main face, but quite often it's cool and foggy here (as well as in most of the coastal areas) while inland it is scorching.

Driving directions

Coming from the south (San Francisco Bay Area), take US-101 north to Petaluma, exit East Washington St. and follow it west through town. Washington St. will turn into Bodega Ave. and then into Valley Ford Rd. before connecting with CA-1. Go north

Number of problems by difficulty

VB	V0	V1	V2	V3	V4	V5	V6	V7	V8	V9	V10	≥V11
1	4	2	1	3	2	3	1	4	0	1	0	0

on CA-1. about 18 miles (about nine miles north of Bodega Bay) to the CA-116 (River Rd.)/CA-1 intersection just south of Jenner.

Coming from the north (Santa Rosa area) on US-101, exit at Mark West Springs Rd./River Rd. and head west on River Rd. for about 15 miles to Guerneville and the CA-116 intersection. Continue west on River Rd./CA-116 for about 12 miles toward CA-1 and Jenner. Just before (south of) Jenner you'll come to the CA-1 intersection.

From the CA-116 (River Rd)/CA1 intersection just south of Jenner turn north onto CA-1. Drive for 2.3 miles (through the town of Jenner) to the parking area in a pullout on the right (east) side of CA-1.

Coming from north of Jenner on CA-1, set your odometer at Skaggs Springs Rd./CA-1 intersection (south of Annapolis and Gualala) and drive south on CA-1 for 25.7 miles to the parking area in a pullout on the left (east) side of CA-1 about one mile north of the town of Jenner. GPS for the trailhead at the parking lot: 38.455267 -123.1328

Approach

Super Slab can be seen above the pullout, just a two to three minute uphill hike. Don't make the mistake of hiking to the rock just south of Super Slab, it looks similar but only has a few boulder problems and a toprope.

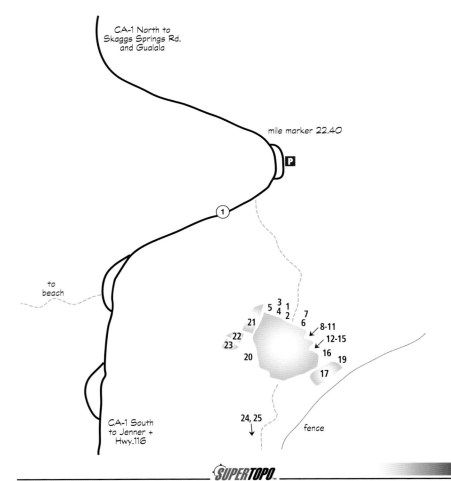

Super Slab

1. Super Slab V6★★★★ Sit start under mini roof on a left hand, three finger gaston pocket and a chunky right hand edge and pull out over the slopey lip of roof onto slab. FA: Marcos Nunez, 90s.

2. Abalone V7★★★ Same sit start as #1 but instead of pulling over the lip onto slab, traverse left along the lower lip/sloper rail to no-hands corner on left side. V6/V7 if you traverse the upper lip (V7 backwards).

3. Super Abalone V8★★★★ Sit start under the far right side of mini roof on a left hand side-pull edge and a right hand rectangular pinch in a tiny crack. Traverse the sloper lip up and left past #1 into #2 to finish. Heel and toe-hook sloper madness. V7/V8 if you traverse the upper lip from #1 to the left (V8 backwards). FA: Chris Summit, 90s.

4. Doctor Octopus V5★★★ Sit start under right side of mini roof (same as #3), then climb out overhang and pull yourself onto the slab to the right of #1 to finish.

5. V3★★ Sit start same as #3 and #4, then pull out right onto slabby face over bushes. Traverse up and right, then go up the V1 slabby face/arête. V1 if you stand start high.

6. Step Ladder V1★★ Low sit start (same as #6) on good edges, then pull yourself up over the bulge and top out on the slab. Follow 5.0 (#8) slab corner to top of crag.

7. Bologna V4★★ Sit start on the left side of short overhanging face (same as #6) and traverse right along the slopey upper lip to the top of #1. Top out slab to finish.

8. The Slab VB★★★ Stand start to high slabby 5.2X face/corner. The first moves are the hardest. Top out on the summit of Super Slab, then climb down the 5.0R backside.

9. Sea Dragon V4★★ Stand start in the corner (#8), then traverse left around arête (#12) into next corner (#13), then up left along rail to same topout as #16.

10. Superconductor V5★★ Same start as #9 and same traverse left around arête (#12) to corner (#13), then traverse up and left along rail to #16 but don't top out. Instead match small crimper edge in center of face and finish on far left side same as #14.

11. Renegades of Funk V9★★ Same start as #9 and #10 to the corner (#13), then do a funky drop down maneuver into the sit start of #14 and #15. Do #15 to finish.

❏ **12. Mouse Crack V0★★★** Arête/Corner. Stand start on face/arête right of corner (#13). Good slot pocket and edges lead up and left into corner crack and onto slab. Either down climb left (5.4R) or pull over final bulge 5.7X onto high slab to top.

❏ **13. Yogi Mantel V2★★** Sit start below corner on big sloper the same as #14 and #15, then mantle sloper up into corner and into crack (#12) to finish.

❏ **14. Bulls on Parade V7★★** Sit start with low right hand slot pocket and left hand edge or sloper. Traverse low and left along horizontal crack under small roof to a hard crux at the freshly broken horn shaped hold. Finish on the far left side. **Bull Horn V6:** sit start on the broken horn into the same left finish. FA: Shawn Rogers, 90s.

❏ **15. Over the Hill V8★★** Same sit start as #14, traverse the crack past the crux at the broken horn then go up via small edges into #16 to finish. **Happy Birthday V7:** sit start Bull Horn into #16 to finish.

❏ **16. Dragonslayer V3★★** Stand start with the obvious small left hand crimp edge in the center of the face and right hand edge/ arête. Go up face/arête.

❏ **17. Chuck Norris V7★★** Stand start with right hand pocket and left hand edge. Make a move up to the lip, then traverse the lip to the right to finish on V1 crack in corner.

❏ **18. Numb Chuck V7★★** Same start as #17 but traverse left (instead of right) into #19.

❏ **19. The Virgin V0★★** Stand start, then diagonal up and left past a good jug to the topout. **V1 Direct Variaiton:** Go straight up the awkward, slabby, shallow dihedral/arête to a semi highball topout.

❏ **20. Not So Super Slab V0★★★** Stand start in the center of slab face and go up. Classic. V1 Traverse the base of the slab in either direction. The low start is V1. FA: Mark Howe, 80s.

❏ **21. Gargoyle V3★★** Stand start in mini cave (often overgrown) and traverse up and left along lip of overhanging boulder above slab boulder. Sketchy landing, pumpy.

❏ **22. V0★** Sit start short (5 ft. tall) splitter crack.

❏ **23. VB★★** Stand start on left side of short (7 ft. tall) boulder opposite #22. Go up slab face.

The Overlook

❏ **24. Crack Pot V0R★★** Diagonal crack to arête/ slab finish. V1 Low start in corner/crack down and right of slab start.

❏ **25. Holding Face 5.10★★** Short toprope.

River Mouth

Number of problems: **10-20**

Rock: **Schist**

Difficulty: **VB-V7**

The mouth of the Russian River opens wide at Goat Rock State Beach with seals, surfers, sightseers, and rock climbers all enjoying the many wonders of this incredible place. The driftwood-covered beach on the north side of the river mouth has two boulders on opposite ends that offer about five to ten problems each and two opposite styles of climbing: slab and steep. The schist boulder closest to the river mouth called The River Mouth Boulder has sandy landings and slabby problems from 5.6-V1 (sometimes the sand covers the rock) and the Fishhead Boulder on the north end of the beach has steeper problems from V0-V7.

Fishead Classics: Fishead Traverse V6 (northwest face) and **Fishface V5** (north face) on the Fishhead Boulder.
River Mouth Classic: **Seal Crack V0-** on the North Face of the River Mouth Boulder.

Driving Directions/Approach

About two miles north of the CA-116/CA-1 intersection on CA-1 (Pacific Coast Hwy.) just north of the last buildings in Jenner park in the turnouts on the west side of CA-1. across from Super Slab. Hike the steep trail downhill to the boulders on the beach or park in a smaller turnout on the west-side of CA-1 about one more mile north (about three miles north of CA-116/CA-1) for the direct hike to the harder problems on the Fishhead Boulder.

Rocks near the River Mouth. Photo by Jerry Dodrill.

Damon Monjure on Fishhead Traverse (V6). Photo by Logan Fessler

Goat Rock

Number of problems: 55

Rock: Blue and Green Schist

Difficulty: VB-V10, mostly V0-V6

Angie Corwin on Pelican Arête (V0R)

The Sunset Boulders at Goat Rock State Park lie in a quiet pasture overlooking a peaceful stretch of beach off the side of the Pacific Coast Hwy. The rocks are close enough to the ocean that you can hear waves crash and far enough from the road to forget about it. A secluded beach is close by and provides a nice place to have a picnic, take a walk, and play in the sand. That's if you are willing to hike down the steep hill from the boulders. These rocks were the first climbing area on the Sonoma Coast and the first place where myself and a lot of other local climbers took off our harnesses and bouldered for the first time. Once you go there you'll see why. Two obvious spires rise out of the grassy field and are surrounded by six 10 to 15 foot tall boulders. The smaller of the two spires, Ram Rock, is only about 30 feet tall. It is a perfect place for beginners to toprope or for experts to highball, making it popular with everyone. In fact, this is the most popular crag on the Sonoma Coast so there is almost a guarantee that there will be a climber or two (or ten) out there on every sunny weekend from here to eternity. However, weekdays are pretty mellow, with most people living too far away for an afternoon jaunt. The boulder problems are mostly short to medium length, moderate to hard difficulty, slightly overhanging technical masterpieces. The stone is blue/green schist, which is crimpy, sharp, and (usually) solid with good in-cut edges and slopers. In a few places you can see ruby red garnets stuck to the surface of the rock. The stone is also uniquely polished in some places. A popular legend is that this polishing is from bison and woolly mammoths that used the boulders as giant backscratchers in the late Pleistocene era.

About the rock

An even mix of overhanging, vertical, and slabby schist. There are also a few cracks. Some problems top out at about 30 feet so toproping is an option from bolt anchors on top. A 5.6R slab face must be soloed or lead climbed on traditional gear to reach the top or to descend any of the boulder problems on Ram Rock (the main spire).

Number of problems by difficulty

VB	V0	V1	V2	V3	V4	V5	V6	V7	V8	V9	V10	≥V11
9	8	6	5	9	4	3	4	1	0	0	3	0

When to climb

All year round good conditions can be had at Goat Rock. Winter is generally wetter and colder with lows in the 30s and highs in the 50s. Summer is usually never too hot, but it can be a bit warm some days with highs in the upper 80s. Many times it is foggy and cool in the 60s when all nearby inland areas are sweltering.

*Access concerns/special notes

The Sunset Boulders in Goat Rock State Park are a popular place for hiking, picnicking, bird watching, archaeological studying, and—of course—rock climbing. With this positive increase in popularity by all user groups also comes a negative increase in the impact on the environment. It is now more important than ever for all visitors to the Sunset Boulders to be careful not to overuse and negatively impact this incredibly wonderful and historic area. Keep your impact to a minimum. Stay on the main established trails, don't harm the flora or fauna (duh), don't climb the rocks with lichen covered faces, stay away from nesting birds or other creatures, and don't overcrowd. If the parking lot is full then consider climbing at one of the other excellent nearby areas. Check out the other areas nearby in this guidebook and in the local North Bay guidebook, Wine Country Rocks. Or at: www.winecountryrocks.com.

Driving directions

Coming from the (south) San Francisco Bay area take US-101 north to Petaluma, exit East Washington St. and follow it west through town. Washington St. will turn into Bodega Ave. and then into Valley Ford Rd. before connecting with CA-1. Go north on CA-1. Go about 17 miles (about eight miles north of Bodega Bay) to the left turn for Goat Rock State Park.*

Coming from the (north) Santa Rosa area on US-101, exit Mark West Springs Rd./River Rd. and head west on River Rd. for about 15 miles to Guerneville and the CA-116 intersection. Continue west on River Rd./CA-116 for about 12 miles toward CA-1 and Jenner. Just before Jenner you'll come to the CA-1 intersection and a bridge over the Russian River. Turn left (south) onto CA-1, go over the bridge and drive one mile to the right turn for Goat Rock State Park.*

*After turning off of CA-1 onto Goat Rock Rd. drive 0.25 miles to the parking in large pullouts on the left (southwest) side of the road.

Approach

Follow the obvious trails downhill toward the smaller, closer, rock outcroppings in the grassy field.

Mammoth Rock   Ram Rock

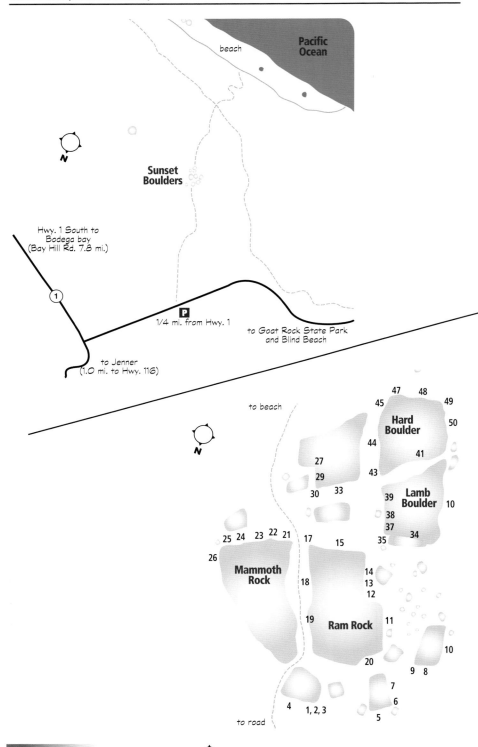

Jason's Boulder (Wet in winter)

❏ **1. Warm-up Traverse V0**★★ Start on right side of small overhanging boulder and traverse along the lip up and left to the far left side.

❏ **2. Jason Lives V6**★★ Sit start on right side and traverse the face to the left, staying below the lip to the center of the short overhanging face, then link up into #4. FA: Jason Campbell, early 1990s.

❏ **3. Jason Dies V6**★★ Same sit start as #2 and same traverse across the face to the center, but rather than going up into #4, continue traversing left to finish on the far left side. FA: Shawn Rogers, 1990s.

❏ **4. V4**★★ Sit start in center of face.

Heel-hooker Boulder

❏ **5. Heel-hooker Traverse V3**★★★ Sit start on the far left side on either boulder and then traverse (hint: heel-hook) along the lip of the steep roof to the right and down around the arête to finish traversing the vertical V0 face.

❏ **6. V1**★★ Sit Start short steep arête.

❏ **7. V0-**★★ Left or Right Sit Starts – Short vertical face over flat, grassy landing.

Bulge Boulder

❏ **8. The Bulge V2**★★ Sit start in center of short roof/face pull out and over to topout.

❏ **9. The Bitch V5**★★ Sit start on left or right (usually done from left to right) traverse along the roof/face, staying below the lip around the corner/arête crux.

❏ **10. V3**★★ Stand or sit start on a slopey face on the right side of the Bitch Boulder.

Odessa Ladinsky on Sunset Traverse (V2).

Ram Rock (5.6R/X Up/Down)

❏ **11. Sunset Face** V0R/X★★★ Start off rock pedestal or on the rocky ground below and climb high up over this treacherous rocky landing on slick, delicate thin slab moves to the committing finish. Toprope-able from bolt anchors.

❏ **12. 5.8R/X★★** Start in corner on short but perfect lie-back crack and go up face/corner to the top. Toprope with a mix of gear, bolts and long slings.

❏ **13. 5.7R/X★★** Slab/crack/face left of #14. Start in the same perfect lie-back crack as #12 and go up right along thin crack and topout left of #14.

❏ **14. Sunset Slab** 5.6R/X★★★★ Sunset Slab 5.6R/X Start off rocky ground and climb up the slabby face to the left of the arête/edge. This is the easiest way up/down boulder and can be toproped. V0 Stand start on short vertical face down and right of the start of #14 and left of Pelican Arête (#16). Go up face onto slab (#14) to finish.

❏ **15. Ram Face** V0★★★ Face to slab.

❏ **16. Ram Traverse** V2★★ Start anywhere on Ram Rock and traverse the entire rock in either direction. Some slightly high sections but the crux is close to the ground.

❏ **17. Pelican Arête** V0R★★★★ Stand start. Ascend sculpted highball arête. Good toprope.

❏ **18. Killer Crack** V1R★★★★ Highball face with thin seam/crack splitting it. Good toprope.

❏ **19. Buckets** 5.7R/X★★ Start on slabby bulge and move up onto and (hopefully) over high vertical face over a bad landing. Bring long slings to set up a toprope.

❏ **20. North Face** V0R/X★★ Shady, slabby, highball. Toprope-able with long slings from bolt anchors on top of Sunset Face.

Mammoth Rock

❏ **21. Sunset Traverse** V2★★★★ Traverse the steep south face of Mammoth Rock.

❏ **22. Great White** V1★★★ Stand start in under-cling, go past edges to jug, to top.

❏ **23. Final Exam** V1-V1R/X★★ Stand start under-cling crack to highball face topout. If you topout higher left its V1r. Higher still V1R/X (5.11aTR) or face variations.

❏ **24. Mid Term** V0+★★★ Finger crack on steep polished face.

❏ **25.** V1★★ Stand start on the polished face between the crack and the arête/corner. Go up.

❏ **26.** 5.6★★ Stemming corner on the southwest face to slabby ledges to top. Down climb.

Potato Chip Boulder

☐ **27.** 5.6★★ Short splitter corner crack.

☐ **28.** V7★★ Start in the corner crack (#27) and traverse up right into #29.

☐ **29. Potato Chip Face** V5★★ Stand start right hand on Potato Chip hold and left hand on crimpy gaston go up center of face.

☐ **30. Potato Chip Arête** V3★★ Stand start with left hand on potato chip hold and right hand on mini arête. Go up the right hand arête. Sit start is V4 (same as #31 and #32).

☐ **31. Open Mind** V10★★ Sit start on a low left hand slot pocket and right hand side-pull, then reach up to the "potato chip" crimp with the right hand and do #29 to finish. FA: Kevin Jorgeson, 2002.

☐ **32. Open Heart** V10★★ Same start as #31 up to the "potato chip" crimp with the right hand, but rather than going up like #31 instead traverse left into the corner crack (#27) to finish. FA: Dave Wallach, 2000.

☐ **33.** 5.7★★ Stand start short vertical face.

Angie Corwin on Rock Scar (V3).

Lamb Boulder

❏ **34. The Lamb** V0+★★ Thin crack/slab face above flat rocky landing.

❏ **35. The Speciialist** V4★★ Sit start on rock with hands matching under-cling flake on short over-hanging face, then pull over the lip onto the left side of the slab and topout. V5 Low sit start using side-pull at base of overhang below V-slot on #37.

❏ **36.** V5★★ Same sit start as #35 Low and #37, then go up the center of the overhang between the v-slot on #37 to the left and the under-cling on #35 to the right. Then continue traversing up right along the lip into the topout on the prow.

❏ **37. Skull Cracker** V1★★★ Stand start on shelf/horn above overhang and pull a hard reach move over a pointy rock. The hazardous rock is just far enough back that you don't usually hit it when you fall but if you were to pitch off backwards then it could live up to it's name.

If you're a klutz, wear a helmet. V2 Low sit start at base of overhang same as #35 on side-pull and do a move up to the V-slot, then up into the stand start.

❏ **38.** V4★★ Stand start same as Skull Cracker (#37), then angle up left into the top of #39. V5 Sit start same as #35 Low.

❏ **39. Rock Scar** V3★★★ Stand or sit start just right of arête on an in-cut edge and go up left hand lie-back to rock scar jug and top out.

❏ **40. Demolition Man** V6★★ Start same as #39, then traverse right into #37. Or start #37 and traverse left into the no-hands corner. **Demolition Specialist** V7: Same start as Demolition Man, then traverse right into The Specialist (#35) to finish.

Hard Boulder

❏ **41. Holy Schist V3**★ Sit start short overhang in tight chimney/gully.

❏ **42. V0**★ Face in gully between #41 + #43.

❏ **43. Hard Arête V2**★★ Stand start left side of arête. Awkward one-move wonder.

❏ **44. V4**★★ Stand start on small side-pull edges. Go up into V-slot topout. V5 Sit start.

❏ **45. Hard Right V4**★★ Stand start on left hand diagonal sloper rail. Traverse up right. V0- Start just left of #45 and right of #47 and go up good high juggy slab face.

❏ **46. Hard Left V4**★★ Stand start on the left side of a line of good crimper edges in the middle of #47 and do a hard move up and left into #48 to topout.

❏ **47. Hard On Traverse V6 or V10**★★★ Stand or sit start on the right side of the main overhanging southwest face. Traverse the line of good crimper edges to the left into the start of #46, then make the move on #46 up and left to better holds, then continue traversing down and left across the steep face to the jugs on the start of #49 and step off. **V10 Variation:** Don't do the move up and left on #46, instead continue traversing past #46 and past a hard crux on under-cling side-pull crimpers into the same finish. FA: Marcos Nunez, early 90s.

❏ **48. Hard Up V2**★★★★ Stand start on gastons and go up right along mini corner/arête. V3 Sit start on a low, in-cut, wafer thin, left hand pinch lay-back and a right hand edge and do a few tenuous moves up into the stand start. Center of steep face.

❏ **49. V1**★★ Stand start on a left hand horn and right hand edge and go up past V-slot pocket high over rock landing.

❏ **50. Viagra V3**★★ Stand start same as #49, then diagonal up left over rocky landing. Die Hard V7 (AKA Dirk Diggler) Do the V6 Hard On into #50 finish.

Blind Beach

Remember the movie Goonies? The final scene of the movie when the pirate ship sets sail was filmed at Goat Rock looking south toward Blind Beach. The official parking for the trail to Blind Beach is 0.25 mile down Goat Rock Rd past the parking for Sunset Boulders. The unofficial parking would be in the huge parking lot between the north and south coves next to Goat Rock at the bottom of Goat Rock Rd (Goat Rock itself is CRUMBLY, DANGEROUS and ILLEGAL TO CLIMB. Don't waste your time.) Either park at the official parking and hike downhill on a fairly good trail for five to ten minutes to the beach (and the Boulders) or park in the unofficial parking lot and hike south down the flat, sandy beach for about the same five to ten minutes to the obvious 30 to 40-foot pile of rocks on the beach in the middle of the south cove. Best at low tide.

❏ **51. Mussel Man Traverse V4**★★★ Usually done from left to right into #52 to finish.

❏ **52. Goonies V2**★★ Stand start in center of face and go up and right into #53 to finish.

❏ **53. V0**★ Stand start chimney/arête-V1 Sit.

❏ **54. Blind Beach Traverse 5.6**★ Traverse slabby base of big rock in either direction.

❏ **55. 5.8R/X**★★ Either highball this 30-foot slab climb, then down climb it or lead it with the one old bolt on the face. On top there is (was) at least one old bolt anchor.

Pomo Canyon

Number of problems: **15**

Rock: **Schist**

Difficulty: **V0-V8**

Pomo Canyon Campground is found in a lush canyon of fern-covered hills and is shrouded by a thick redwood forest. The 40-foot schist crag known as Pomo Rock is a five to ten-minute hike up the main creek from the campground. The popular Pomo Trail starts at the campground and heads west over the hills for about 2.5 miles to Shell Beach where the local Pomo Indian tribe used to meet and trade with other tribes of the area.

Pomo Rock is not on the Pomo Trail, it is in the creek to the south of it. Most of the boulder problems are found in the Pomo Cave on the back of Pomo Rock and are steep test-pieces with easier, yet highball topouts. Hang and drop finishes are legit in the cave when the topouts are dirty and because most of the cruxes are right off the ground.

About the rock

A 40-foot tall schist crag surrounded by a few short steep boulders. The Pomo Cave has about ten good, steep, hard problems over a rocky creek bed. Pads are good.

When to climb

The creek hits most of the problems in the cave in winter but the long Pomosapien Traverse on the main face of Pomo Rock is usually dry and good all year (unless it's raining, of course). The traverse also has easier sections to do, as well as better landings than the problems in the cave. During the wet months of winter the campground is closed and the three-quarter

Charlie Barrett on Ganesh (V7).

mile dirt road that leads from Willow Creek Rd. to the campground parking lot is also closed. It is possible to park on Willow Creek Rd. and walk in but this takes twice as long, about 15 to 25 minutes.

Driving directions

Coming from the San Francisco Bay area (south), take US-101 north to Petaluma, exit East Washington St. and follow it west through town. Washington St. will turn into Bodega Ave. and then into Valley Ford Rd. before connecting with CA-1. Go north on CA-1 about 18 miles (about nine miles north of Bodega Bay) to the right turn for *Willow Creek Rd.

Coming from the Santa Rosa area (north) on US-101, exit Mark West Springs Rd./River Rd. and head west on River Rd.

Number of problems by difficulty

VB	V0	V1	V2	V3	V4	V5	V6	V7	V8	V9	V10	≥V11
0	0	2	1	1	4	3	2	1	0	0	0	0

for about 15 miles to Guerneville and the CA-116 intersection. Continue west on River Rd./CA-116 for about 12 miles toward CA-1 and Jenner. Just before Jenner you'll come to the CA-1 intersection and a bridge over the Russian River. Turn left (south) onto CA-1, go over the bridge and turn left onto Willow Creek Rd.*

*Willow Creek Rd. starts on CA-1 from the south side of the bridge over the Russian River at a place called Bridgehaven. Turn off CA-1 onto Willow Creek Rd. and drive 2.7 miles to the Pomo Canyon Campground on the right. Drive through the gate and down the half-mile dirt road to the parking lot. The gate and the campground are closed

in winter but you can still park outside and walk in. GPS for the trailhead at the parking lot: 38.424917, -123.0652

Approach

From the parking lot follow the main trail through the campground, staying south of the main Pomo Trail. The campground trail will end at the last campsite but continue following smaller trails up the creek. Follow the creek uphill, staying on the left side until you see the bouldering on the moss covered, 40-foot tall Pomo Rock. Total hiking time from parking lot is 10 to 15 minutes.

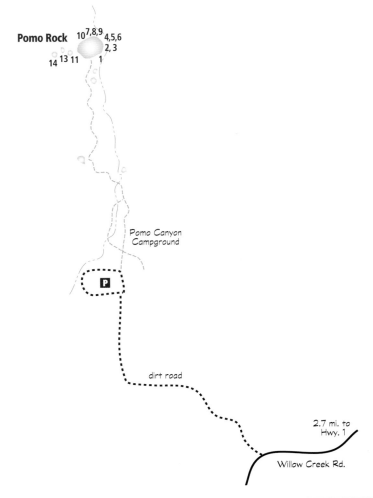

Pomo Rock

❑ **1. Pomosapien Traverse** V4★★★ Stand or sit start right of a knee high boulder in a crevice at the base of the crag. Usually done from right to left, uphill. Left half is V1. The stand start on the far right side is V5.

❑ **2. Chalupa** V1★★★ Stand start on jug rail and make moves up over bulge onto highball slab to finish. Once on the slab, make moves up and right into the same 5.6R/X topout as #3–#5. Often dirty, but all there. The sit start on small edges below the jug rail is V2.

❑ **3. Ganesh** V7★★★★ Stand start on a sloper left hand edge and a tiny right hand crimp in the center of the overhanging face just right of #2 and try to go up. Same highball V0R/X finish as #2, #4 and #5. If you finish on #6, the problem is V8.

❑ **4. Middle Ground** V4★★★ High stand start with right hand on crux edge of #5 and left hand on crux edge of #3. Go up into the same finish as #5. (V0R/X slab topout.) **Solid Ground V5:** do the same start as #4 but traverse right into #6 finish.

❑ **5. Streamline** V5★★★★ Stand start arête. Same 5.6R/X slab finish as #2, #3 and #4. The sit start is V6. The lower holds on sit start are usually wet from November to July.

❑ **6. Work of Art** V6★★ Stand start same as arête (#5) but just after the crux angle up and right over rocky landing into #9 or #10 to topout. The sit start is V7.

❑ **7. Pomo Cave Traverse** V5★★ Stand start same as #5 and #6, but traverse to the right past a hard crux into #9 or #10 to finish. The sit start is V6.

❑ **8. Ohaus** V4★★★ Stand start just right of #5 on a pockety sloper and follow the diagonal seam up and left into the same finish as #5.**V5 Variation:** same start as #8 but after crux go up and right into #6.

❑ **9. Pomo Roof** V3★★★ Stand start in mini cave on good juggy pockets and go straight backwards out horizontal roof into the highball V1R/X Pomo Face to finish.Stand start in hole for the V1R/X highball finish of Pomo Roof.

❑ **10. Tug of War With Cyclops** V1★★ Start under far right side of cave and top out on slab to finish. Step off or angle up and left into top of #9 (5.7R/X). Stand start is V0.

❑ **11. Lucky Leprechaun** V2★★ Sit or stand start and go up left hand arête. **Lucky Nuggs V5 Variation:** sit start on the left arête (#11), then traverse the lower line of holds to the right into the sit start of #12 to finish.

❑ **12. Fondle Your Nuggs** V4★★ Sit start on horizontal rail and do a couple powerful moves up to and over the right arête. **Fondle Your Leprechaun V4 Variation:** sit start #13, then traverse up and left into the topout of the left arête (#11) to finish.

❑ **13. Black Hands** V6★★ Low stand start. Go up overhanging prow shaped boulder in alcove. V4 High start. Topout optional.

❑ **14.** V5★★ Stand start with right hand lie-back edge and left hand edge and bust a move up and left to a long in-cut two hand edge on a mossy slab. Match up and drop off. Right side of the big overhanging boulder uphill from #11-#13.

❑ **15.** Projects.

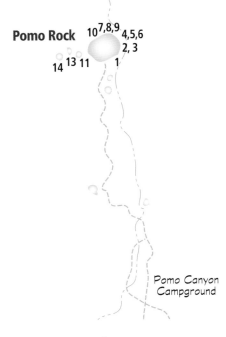

Pomo Rock   10 ^{7,8,9} 4,5,6
                        2, 3
14 13 11   1

Pomo Canyon
Campground

Marshall Gulch

Problems: 10-20

Rock: **Graywacke Sandstone**

Difficulty: **V0-V6/8**

Kevin Jorgeson does first ascent of The Cave (V6).

Water polished graywacke sandstone over sandy landings on a popular beach close to Bodega Bay. Oh yes it is nice but it is also quite moody. A low tide is needed for most of the problems here to be dry, preferably a low tide in the afternoon when the west-facing cliffband gets direct sunlight to finish drying any damp nooks and crannies. Also, the sand levels fluctuate all year. Low sand is good for the low hard sit start to The Cave but it is unpredictable. There is a lot of intermediate terrain over mostly sandy landings. Hang and drop finishes are the norm since most of the bouldering is done along the base of a long 40-foot-tall cliffband with a dirty topout. Hundreds of feet of traversing can be done on good jugs.

Classics: **The Gulch Traverse V0-V4/5, Marshall Cave V4** (left), V6 (direct) or V8 (low stand).

Driving Directions/Approach

On CA-1 (Pacific Coast Hwy.) about 2.6 miles north of Bay Hill Rd. (the last major road on the north side of Bodega Bay). Coming from the north it's about five miles south of the Sunset Boulders at Goat Rock State Park. Look for the sign and the large pullout with a trail heading south into the gulch. The bouldering is all along the base of the cliffs south of the gulch and most of it requires a low tide.

Dillon Beach

Problems: 10-20

Rock: Schist

Difficulty: V0-V5

Kenny Ariza on the Bouncer (V5).

Views of Point Reyes and Bodega Head, surfing The Shark Pit at the mouth of Tomales Bay, and the unique slot pocketed schist boulders on the quiet north end of Dillon Beach make the out of the way drive worth it. The large boulder with the rusty old bolt ladder known as the Stud Ladder is the main spot. The wall that faces away from the ocean with the Stud Ladder also has the classic Dillon Beach Traverse (V3) and a lot of good up problems, all of which down climb the slabby 5.7R/X south east arête. The west (ocean) side of the main boulder has a few new highball problems just established during the making of this guide. The landing under the west face is so rocky that two to three pads and one spotter is the minimum to be safe and even then that's only with the hang and drop finishes. With the V0x topouts no amount of pads or spotters will save you.

Classics: **Stud Ladder V1 or V2** (right sit), **Dillon Beach Traverse V3, Bouncer V5,** and **Tribute V4r** (west face).

Driving Directions/Approach

Coming from the (south) San Francisco Bay area take US-101 north to Petaluma, exit East Washington St. and follow it west through town. Washington St. will turn into Bodega Ave. and just before (east of) the tiny town of Two Rock turn left onto Tomales Rd. (following signs to Dillon Beach).

Coming from the (north) Santa Rosa area take US-101 south to Cotati, exit onto Gravenstein Highway/CA-116 and follow it west out of town toward Sebastopol. After about a mile turn left on Stony Point Rd. and go about two miles to a right turn onto Mecham Rd. and turn right onto Pepper Rd. Follow Pepper Rd for a couple miles to a right turn onto Bodega Ave. Go less than a mile on Bodega Ave. and just before (east of) the tiny town of Two Rock turn left onto Tomales Rd. (following signs to Dillon Beach). From the end of Tomales Rd in the town of Tomales take a right onto CA-1 and go into downtown to the left turn onto Dillon Beach Rd. Drive about four miles to Dillon Beach passing Elephant Rock* Once down at Dillon Beach a $5 parking fee is required for the parking lot. Park in the far north end, hike through the sand dunes and walk north along the flat sandy beach for about five minutes to the obvious rocks on the north end of Dillon Beach.

The awesome looking sandstone spires known as Elephant Rock (off the side of the road just before Dillon Beach) are private property and mostly chossy.

Stinson Beach

Problems: 25

Rock: Serpentine and Greywacke Sandstone

Difficulty: V0-V11

On the southern end of the popular yet mellow Stinson Beach in Marin County are a few fine beach boulders. Are You Experienced and its stout neighbor The Old Man are the standouts. Are You Experienced is the smaller of the two main boulders and sports most of the hard problems. It sits against the base of the hill farther from the ocean than any of the other boulders on the beach and is therefore climbable more often. The Old Man is high with a long weird traverse and only a few boulder problems/topropes. It is closer to the ocean and gets wet every day at high tide, either a little or a lot. Scattered all around are more good boulders with a variety of problems. Local bouldering guru Russ Bobzien brought hard bouldering to the North Bay when he did the test-pieces on the Are You Experienced boulder in the 1980s. His technical endurance traverse called Are You Experienced and the powerful Manitou V11 were on the cutting edge of difficulty when they were put up. Even today they are some of the most difficult problems in the Bay Area. Russ helped open the eyes of other local boulderers of that era (myself included) to what was possible on our local rock. Have you ever been experienced?

About the rock

The biggest rock (20 to 25 ft.), called The Old Man, is high enough to deserve a toprope for a few of the problems on its main face. Old bolts on top and cracks for gear with long slings can be used.

Charlie Barrett clings onto Manitou (V11).

The shorter (15 to 20 ft.) and steeper Are You Experienced boulder has the highest concentration of problems on the beach and also the hardest problems from V2 to V11. To the south of Are You Experienced is a fun boulder with about five problems from V0 to V3. To the north of The Old Man and Old Woman are about five to ten other good boulders with about 10 to 20 more problems.

When to climb

The wet months in winter are the most unpredictable. Storms in the Pacific push huge swells up onto the beach and all around the boulders. The big waves also deposit debris like driftwood and small rocks under the base of the problems. Don't let this scare you away. Quite often in the

Number of problems by difficulty

VB	V0	V1	V2	V3	V4	V5	V6	V7	V8	V9	V10	≥V11
1	4	6	3	2	4	2	1	1	0	1	1	2

middle of winter our wonderful California climate will give us a perfect warm and sunny day with a nice cool breeze that dries the rock amazingly fast. Every day, all year long, high tide floods the bottom of most of the boulders except Are You Experienced, which is far enough away from the ocean that it usually only gets wet at high, high tides. Check a tide chart if you don't want to get stuck on the more difficult problems of the Are You Experienced boulder while you wait the few hours for high tide to go down. The sand levels around the base of the boulders also changes but on a much slower seasonal schedule. Usually in winter the sand is lower so the problems are higher, while in summer the sand is higher so the problems are a bit lower. Sometimes the higher sand level will cover the low starts to a few of the problems on The Old Man and Old Woman boulders, making them un-climbable for a few months. Summer at the beach boulders for the most part is like paradise, with sandy landings, sunbathing, surfing and relief from the hotter inland temps. Climbing on the coast is always a gamble whatever time of year but hey, even on the worst day when you get hit by a wave, or rained on, or your pad decides to go surfing without you, it's still hard to get bummed out being in one of the most beautiful places on earth.

Driving Direcitons

Stinson Beach has its own parking lot off CA-1 (Shoreline Hwy.) just north of the general store and the main intersection in the small town of Stinson Beach in Marin County. On US-101/CA-1 north of San Francisco about 3.5 miles north of the Golden Gate Bridge take the exit for CA-1 (Shoreline Hwy..) North/Stinson Beach. Keep following the signs for CA-1 (Shoreline Hwy.) north/Stinson Beach. Make sure to stay left at Tam Junction and the turn for the Panoramic Hwy.. About 12 twisty miles from the US-101/CA-1 intersection you'll come to the small town of Stinson Beach. On the right you'll pass the general store and the next left turn will be for the parking lot to Stinson Beach. Enter the parking lot and go as far south as you can before parking. On popular beach-going holidays like Memorial Day and 4th of July the dirt parking lot further south is usually open, making the five-minute walk only two minutes.

Approach

From the south end of the dirt parking lot, walk along the beach in the sand to the obvious boulders at the far south end of Stinson Beach. Hike time: 5 to 10 minutes.

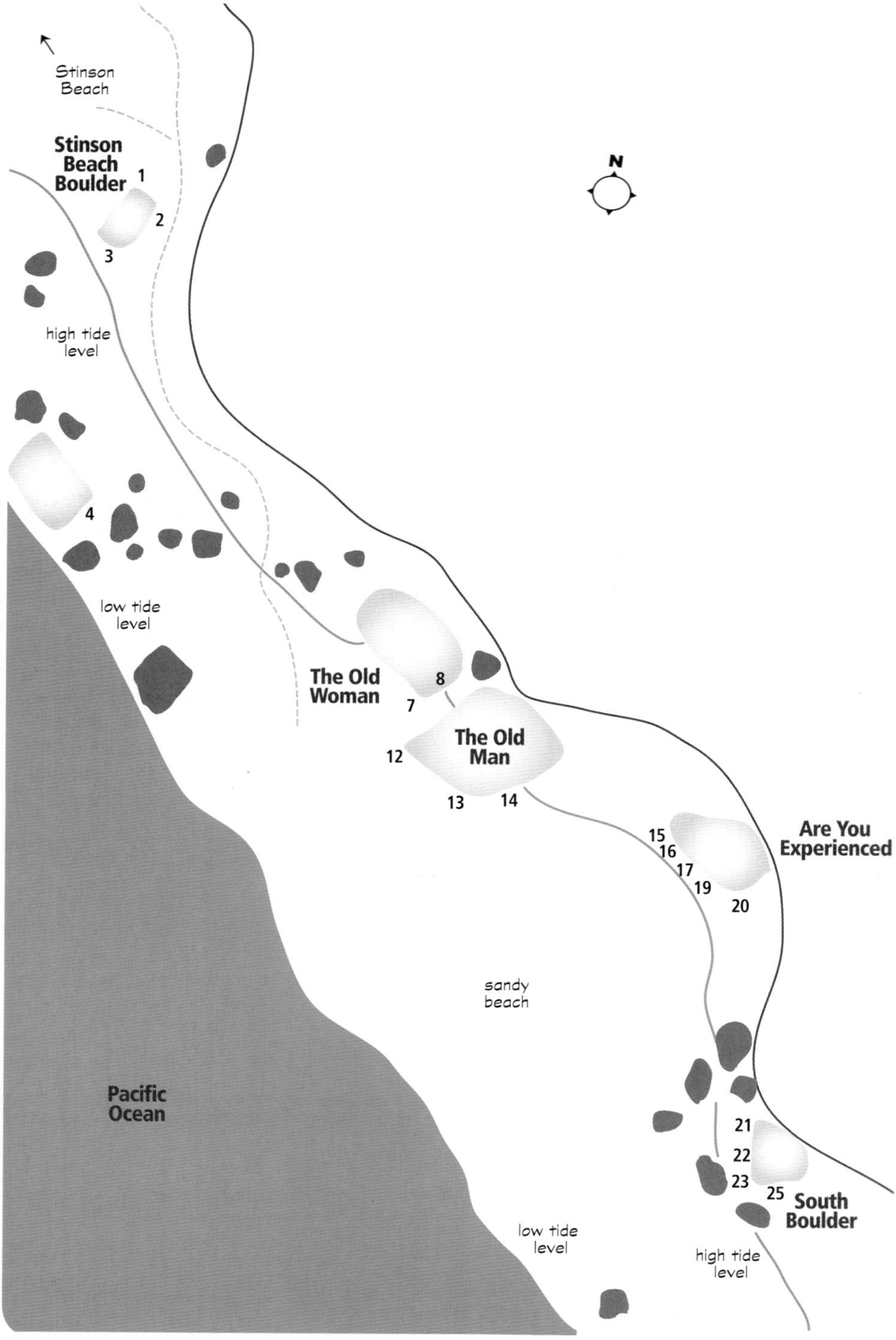

Stinson
Beach

**Stinson
Beach
Boulder** 1

2

3

high tide
level

low tide
level

4

N

**The Old
Woman** 8

7

12

**The Old
Man**

13   14

15
16
17
19

**Are You
Experienced**

20

sandy
beach

21

22

23

25 **South
Boulder**

**Pacific
Ocean**

low tide
level

high tide
level

Lisa Quigg on Problem 1 (V1) Photo by James Hosler. www.hoslerphotography.com

Mike Papciak at on the High Tide Traverse. Photo by Jim Thornburg.

Stinson Beach Boulder

❏ **1. V0★★** Steep slabby face.

❏ **2. V1★★** Sit or stand start.

❏ **3. V1-V3★★** Sit of stand start overhang.

Low Tide Boudler

❏ **4. V3/4★★** Stand or sit start (sand height dependent), traverse up and left to topout.

❏ **5. V1/2★★** Steep face left of #4.

The Beach Boulders

❏ **6. VB-V1★★** Various problems.

The Old Woman Boulder

❏ **7. Old Woman Arête V0★★★** Stand start left hand arête. Good warm-up. V1 Sit start.

❏ **8. V6★★** Stand start the center of the steep face right of the arête #7. Low sand, low start.

❏ **9. V2★★** Stand start the main face right of #8 and go up dark solid rock on good in-cuts.

❏ **10. V3★★** Sit start on steep slab face. A pad is good for the rocky landing.

The Old Man Boulder

❏ **11. High Tide Traverse V5★★** Traverse the north face. Extra fun at high tide when the water is splashing under your feet. **Old Man Traverse V6/7:** Traverse the west face of The Old Man Boulder in either direction between problems #12 and #14. **V7/8 Variation:** from right to left into the High Tide Traverse.

❏ **12. V4★★** Arête. Jump off or highball/ solo topout.

❏ **13. The Old Man V1-V5★★★** Sand height dependent. Low sand, low start: V5. High sand, high start: V1. Stand start in the center of the steep west face and bust moves up into the highball V0X solo slab topout or down climb/jump.

❏ **14. V0R/X★★** Wide cracks with highball finish.

Are You Experienced Boulder

GPS: 53.5025, -122.635278

❏ **15. Are You Experienced V10★★★** Sit start on the left side, then traverse right across the main face, conserving energy for the final crux. The final crux by itself is a three-star V4 stand start on a left hand sloper meatwrap gaston and a right hand knobby crimp. FA: Russell Bobzien.

❏ **16. V4★★** Stand start left arête/corner. Or V5 Sit start.

❏ **17. Manitou V11★★★** Sit start on left hand side-pull scoop and go up past right hand crimper gaston crux. Mantra Man V11 Sit start same as Manitou but go up using the gaston as a crimper under-cling. Manitou Man V11 Start Manitou finish Mantra Man. FA: Russell Bobzien.

❏ **17b. Little Wing V9★★★** Sit start Mantra Man, go up using the big right hand sloper rail. V7 stand start same as Manitou and Mantra Man. When the sand is low or gone or if you just can't reach the good starting edge, a pad stack or cheat stone is legit.

❏ **18. Central Scrutinizer V4 or V5★★** V5 sit start to direct topout or V4 sit start to right.

❏ **19. Standard Route V2★★★** Stand start on under-cling side-pulls and climb up right into the slabby groove to topout. V3 Sit start on left hand horn.

❏ **20. Smiley Face V5★★★** Stand start on right hand crimper edge. V6 Sit start on sloper.

South Boulder

❏ **21. V1/2★★** Stand start on the left side of face and go up. Down climb or walk down hill.

❏ **22. V1★★** Stand start the seam on the right side of the steep slab face.

❏ **23. V1★★** Sit start arête.

❏ **24. V2/3★★** Start on the right or left and traverse across the base of the rock around the arête (#23). Technical and fun climbing over a slightly rocky landing.

❏ **25. V0★★** Sit or stand start the short juggy overhang.

Mickey's Beach

Problems: 65

Rock: Serpentine and Greywacke Sandstone

Difficulty: V0-V11

Only climbers call this Mickey's Beach—everyone else knows it as Red Rock. Why do climbers call it Mickey's? Who is Mickey? Nobody knows for sure. One of the most believable stories is that Mickey was the name of a guy who fell off of a rock on the beach and died in the 1950s or 60s, the name stuck and there you have it.

The rocks on the north end of the beach form a natural barrier from the popular and sometimes crowded Stinson Beach on the other side. The sheltered strip of sandy beach between the rocky barrier and the northwest face of The Orange Buddha Boulder is one of the most popular nude beaches in Northern California. Either drop your britches and enjoy some real free climbing or feel equally as awkward wearing your clothes and knowing you're too uptight to let it all hang out.

Variety is the spice of life and that is exactly what you can find at Mickey's, maybe not so much the variety of bouldering but more the variety of bouldering experiences.

The environment on the coast is in a constant state of flux and at Mickey's you can actually see changes occur in our lifetime, which geologically speaking is like a blink of time. The Orange Buddha Boulder and a couple of its neighbors used to be on the hillside above the nude beach until sometime in the 1980s when it slid down the hill and came to rest where it is now. The story goes on to say how it was all in one big piece and stayed that way for a short time until one day when it broke

Sean Brady on Problem # 1 (V4).

into pieces in front of a couple of shocked picnickers. Believe it or not. One of the old school beach locals painted DANGER on the overhanging west face of The Orange Buddha Boulder shortly after to warn people not to sit under it and definitely not to climb on it because of its unstable nature. Nobody pays attention. I climb on it but I won't sit under it, as if that makes any sense. Strong Marin County local Russ Bobzien did some of the first and best problems on The Orange Buddha after its arrival. A lot of other new problems have been put up recently since the advent of the modern day crash pad. Russ along with other strong locals like Scott Frye, Mike Papciak, Paul Barrazza, Ken Ariza, Frankie Ocasio, Jim Thornburg, and myself developed new problems on every corner of the beach around the turn of the century and even right up to press time.

Number of problems by difficulty

VB	V0	V1	V2	V3	V4	V5	V6	V7	V8	V9	V10	≥V11
0	2	1	9	5	3	4	4	1	3	2	1	0

About the rock

Steep powerful test-pieces, highball slab classics and a lot of good moderate problems over sandy beach landings, bad rocky landings, or a devious mix of both. A pad is mandatory except for the nude beach side of The Orange Buddha, which usually has some sand. More than one pad is best since a lot of the landings are totally rocky. The holds on the problems are mostly edges, jugs, and an occasional pocket or crack. The texture is usually smooth and polished and quite unique. A lot of the rock on the beach is crumbly choss, so finding the best pieces is the first part of the challenge.

When to climb

Spring, summer, and fall are best. Cold foggy days after a rainstorm or a particularly high tide can sometimes leave a few of the boulders wet for a little longer than most inland bouldering areas. On the other hand, it can also be the perfect place to escape the heat of summer at the other areas. High tide pushes the Pacific Ocean up onto the nude beach and up against the west side of The Orange Buddha Boulder and The Red Boulder, drenching them daily. Luckily they dry quickly, but it is always good to check a tide chart before you come, especially if you want to do the climbs on the nude beach. Don't mind the nude people and they won't mind you. They are always there, summer or winter, and always naked or at least partially naked, playing Frisbee or just hanging out.

Driving Directions

Mickey's Beach is one mile south of the small town of Stinson Beach on CA-1 (Shoreline Highway). North of San Francisco, about 3.5 miles north of the Golden Gate Bridge on US-101/CA-1 take the exit for CA-1 North/Stinson Beach. Make sure to stay left at Tam Junction. Approximately 11.3 miles from the US-101/CA-1 intersection will be the large Red Rock parking lot on the left (west) side of CA-1. Parking log GPS: 37.888783, -122.629617

Approach

From the parking lot, follow the main trail downhill to the beach. About a five-minute hike down the trail and you will be on top of the Main Rock, the popular sport climbing crag at Mickey's Beach. Another couple minutes hike down and right (north) will get you to the nude beach and the Nude Beach Boulders. You'll know when you're there.

Janet Bickford campusing over the Pacific. Photo by Jimmy Liu.

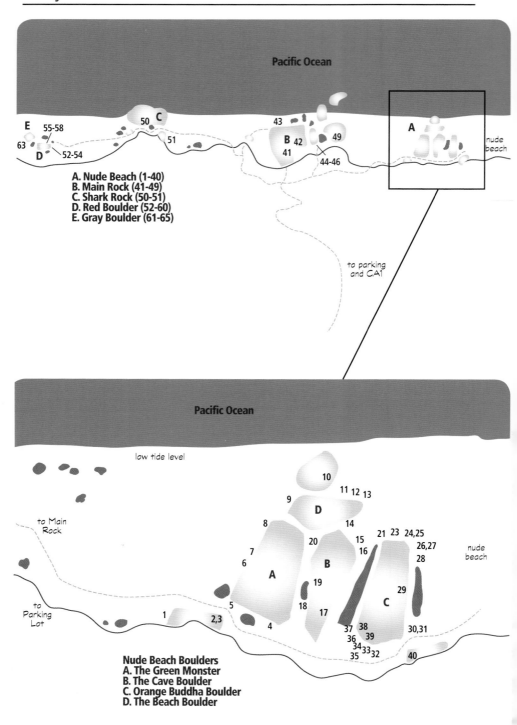

Pacific Ocean

E 55-58
63   52-54
D

50 C
51
43
B 42
41
44-46
49
A
nude beach

A. Nude Beach (1-40)
B. Main Rock (41-49)
C. Shark Rock (50-51)
D. Red Boulder (52-60)
E. Gray Boulder (61-65)

to parking and CA1

Pacific Ocean

low tide level

to Main Rock

to Parking Lot

10
11 12 13
9
D
8
14
7
20
6
A
5
1
2,3
4
19
18
17
15
16
21 23 24,25
26,27
28
29
B
C
37 38
36 39
34 33 32
35
30,31
40
nude beach

Nude Beach Boulders
A. The Green Monster
B. The Cave Boulder
C. Orange Buddha Boulder
D. The Beach Boulder

Trailside Boulder

❏ **1. V4**★★ This traverse is usually done from right to left into #2 to finish.

❏ **2. V2**★★ Sit start on a big right hand under-cling and go straight up face to top of boulder.

❏ **3. V0**★ Stand start on far left side of boulder. Go straight up into the same finish as #2.

The Green Monster

❏ **4. The Red Monster V4**★★ Stand or sit start into highball face. Drop off of jugs at lip or topout the V0X slab. Don't forget you'll have to down climb V0X to get off.

❏ **5. Ah Baloney V9**★★ Stand start on obvious jug down and left of arête. Make moves up and right past arête to topout on a slopey ledge. To descend, down climb and jump for the pads between the boulders at the base.

❏ **6. The Green Monster V3**★★★ Stand start in the center of the main (southwest) face of The Green Monster and go straight up to a ledge about 15 to 20 ft. above the ground. Climb down and left to # 8 to descend. In winter the sand goes down, exposing jagged rocks and making this highball problem even higherball (V3R). The sit start is V4 and V4R in winter.

❏ **7. V5**★★★ Low sit start on left hand lie-back. Traverse up and right into #6 to finish.

❏ **8. V0**★★ Stand start then up face. Topout on ledge then climb back down or traverse off left to nearby rock to descend. V0R Highball in winter when the sand is low.

The Beach Boulder

❏ **9. V1**★ Stand start in the center of the short steep south face. Low tide only. (Hard to reach starting holds in winter when the sand is low.)

The Beach Boulder

❏ **10. V0**★ Sit or stand start up lie-back flake. Low tide. Right of Beach Boulder.

❏ **11. Beach Face** V1★★★ Stand or sit start in the center of an overhanging face just right of the arête.

❏ **12. V2**★★ Same start as #11, then traverse left around arête to the far left side of the boulder in The Cave. V3 Traverse left to right then finish on #11.

❏ **13. Yuji's Dyno** V6★★ Same stand start as #11, then dyno to the top jug.

❏ **14. V0**★★ Stand start bulgy face. Down climb.

The Cave Boulder

❏ **15. V1R**★ Stand start on good holds and angle up and right into highball topout. Much higher in winter when the sand is low (V1R/X). The sit start is V2 (V2R/X with low sand).

❏ **16. Red Tide Traverse** V1★★ Stand start same as #15 but traverse left to a no-hands rest at the base of #17 and step off. Or turn around and go back. Bad landing. Or for an extra thrill, go up into #17 to finish. V2 sit start same as #15.

❏ **17. Red Tide** V0R★★ Highball slab face. To descend, down climb 5.7r slab on backside.

❏ **18. V3**★★ Sit start on small roof. Bust a move up to the lip, then traverse off right and pull onto slab to finish. V4 same sit start then pull straight over lip – direct.

❏ **19. V4**★ Sit start on top of flat top boulder. Short hard pull onto slab.

❏ **20. The Way of the Wah (aka The Cave)** V8★★★ Sit start under huge roof/cave boulder. Pull and heelhook your way out and up onto high face finish. Way good. This is a five-star problem when dry, but it's wet most of the year with a bad landing. V4 Stand start on holds just above the lip and go up high face to top.

Main Rock

Orange Buddha Boulder

❏ **21. Hammerhead** V0★★ Stand start on the corner of the lip of the overhang and yank yourself up and left to the higher lip and topout or traverse farther left around corner to top of #26.

❏ **22. Hammerhead Traverse** V7★★ Same start as #21 but traverse up and right over rock along the jug lip, past a slopey section, then turn the corner and pass #37 + #38 into the topout on #39. Pumpy.

❏ **23. Bound by Tension** V11★★ Sit start on a pair of edges. Head left, climbing on the left side until it possible to reach the blocky edges high on the right side of the arête. FA: Frankie Ocasio, 2006.

❏ **24.** V4★★ Sit start on a flat, two-handed rail just right of #26 and go up edges to the same topout as #26. (The diagonal crack on # 26 is off. Stay on the face to the right.)

❏ **25. Peeping Tom Traverse** V8★★ Same sit start as #24 but make the move up and left into the diagonal crack on #26 and then continue traversing left, staying low all the way to the sit start of #30, then top out # 30 to finish. Requires low sand.

❏ **26.** V1★★★ Stand start diagonal crack on short overhanging face. Top out onto flat top or traverse the juggy lip to the right for a little more pump and a lot more fun. The sit start is V3. Requires low sand.

❏ **27. Great White Traverse** V8★★ Same sit start as #26, then traverse the lip of the overhang right around the corner, then drop down (campus style) into the start of #22. Do #22 to finish. Long and pumpy.

❏ **28.** V4★★ Sit start on a flat jug just left of the sit start for #26 and go straight up face past gastons and under-clings.

❏ **29.** V6★★ Sit start under roof on jugs and pull out onto slopers on the face. Crank past the slopers into the hueco stand start to finish. Hueco stand start: V0.

❏ **30. Grace Face** V5★★ Sit start on diagonal rail and gracefully make your way up this balancey face climb over a good landing squeezed between a couple of bad landings. The stand start is V4.

❏ **31. Orange Buddha Traverse** V3 or V6 or V10★★ **V3-High:** Same stand start as #30. Traverse right into the top of #26 to finish. **V6-Low:** Same sit start as #30. Traverse right, staying low to topout on #26. **Shark Sighting V10:** Sit start same as #30, then do the low variation of the Orange Buddha Traverse into Great White Traverse (#27) to finish. Long and pumpy traverse of nearly the entire Orange Buddha Boulder.

32. Back in the Day V4★★ Sit start on slopey hand rail, make moves straight up past small pocket to topout. 32a: **Buddha** V4 Same start, then traverse up left into #39.

33. Orange Pleasure V4★★★ Sit start on small (but good) flat edges and move up and out overhang into #39 to finish. 33a: V5 Same start, then up right to finish.

34. V4★★ Sit start on a flat left hand gaston and a good right hand edge just left of the sit start to #33. Go straight up past a couple hard moves into #39 to topout. 34a: V5 Link up into #38.

35. Dayo V6★★ Same start as #34, then traverse right past start of #33 into #32.

36. Bodhi Day V9★★ Low sit start just right of the sit start for #37 into #35 to finish.

37. Orange Buddha Arête V8★★★ Sit start low in rocky pit and maneuver yourself up strange arête feature to the top. FA: Russ Bobzien.

38. V2★★ Stand start left of juggy crack (#39) and go up left past a long reach move.

39. V0★★ Stand start at the base of juggy diagonal crack. Follow the crack up and right to topout. Don't pull too hard on the hollow jugs.

40. V3★ Stand or sit vert face on rock north of Buddha. Make moves up, then pull around left to topout and see naked people.

Main Rock

GPS: 37.88865, -122.632483

41. North Face Traverse V1★★ Traverse the slabby base of the Main Rock between the sport climbs Walking a Thin Line 5.10 and the 5.10 corner on the left.

42. The Dream Traverse V4★★★ Traverse from a stand start at the base of the sport climb Dreams of White Porsches to the left past the start of Wet Dreams and Holy Mackerel into #41 to finish. V5 Sit.

43. West Face Traverse V4/5R★★ Traverse the base of the west face between the sport climbs Squid Viscous and Beach Arête. Bad Landing. Climb at low tide.

44. V4★★ Usually done from a sit start on the right to left into #45 to finish.

45. V0★ Stand start on left hand lie-back. Make a move up to in-cut jug, then top out.

46. V1 or V0★★ Arête is V1 (sit or stand start). Crack is V0 (same sit or stand start).

47. V0★★ Short pockety west face.

48. V1R★ West face arête. Bad landing.

Peeper Rock

49. Tool User V6★★ Low start on chest high in-cut edges in gully. Crimp up and right around arête to diagonal rail, then traverse off right and either jump to pads, continue traversing right and down climb, or finish straight up on V0X.

Shark Rock

50. Pool Shark V7★★ Sit start in mini cave over tide pool. V5 edge start.

51. Imaginary Voyage V3★★ Sit start arête on small boulder next to Shark Rock. **Pounce V5:** Stand start face left of #51.

Red Boulder

GPS: 37.8879, -122.63165

52. Cheat Stone Arête V3★★ Stack rocks or pads to reach the first right hand knobby lie-back, then go up arête left of High Rev.

53. High Rev Motor Sports V4★★★ Sit start on good right hand hold on the lip of the under-cut face to the left of Kenny's Arête and go up. High Rev V3 Stand start.

54. Kenny's Arête V4★★★ Stand start highball right hand arête over rocky landing. Red Eye Arête V5 Sit start.

55. V1R/X★★ Stand start left of crack/arête (#56) and right of Kenny's Arête (#54). Steep slab highball face.

56. Red Crack V0★★★ Stand start highball lieback crack/arête.

57. Mirror Image V1★★★ Highball Face. Center of steep, smooth, red slab.

58. Bobblehead V2★★ Sit start to high face/arête right of #57. V0 Stand start.

59. V0★ Crack/Corner. Right of #58.

60. Castaway V4★★ Sit start and up over bulge on backside of boulder.

Grey Boulder

61. Running Man V1★★ Stand start at southwest corner of grey boulder and go up into highball finish. V3 Sit start with right hand in a slot with small wobbly chockstone. Don't use the runningboard ledge for a foothold (if you do it's V2).

62. V3★★ Traverse south face from sit start of #61 to the right and end on no-hands slab. **V3 Variaiton:** Traverse south face from no-hands slab on right to the left into #61.

63. Plumb Line V4★★ Short, powerful sit start in center of south face into reachy highball topout. V1 Stand start on jugs and do big reaches between good holds to the lip, then pull onto slab finish (same as #61) to the tip top of the rock.

64. Yellow Cab Adventure V1R/X★★ Stand start on good holds right of #63 and go up face into highball slab over rock. Bad landing. V2r Low start between rocks.

65. Mr. Clean V1★★ Stand start on rails, crank past good edges and pockets onto slab to finish. Northwest Face. Down climb left.

B. Main Rock (41-49)
C. Shark Rock (50-51)
D. Red Boulder (52-60)
E. Gray Boulder (61-65)

Ring Mountain

Problems: **25**

Rock: **Serpentine**

Difficulty: **VB-V8, mostly V0-V2**

Ring Mountain is a nature preserve with a few hiking/biking trails and two distinct rock formations: Split Rock and Turtle Rock. Split Rock is the obvious slabby rock south of the parking area at the end of Taylor Rd. Turtle is over the hill a short hike to the west. There is also a smaller third formation known as Meatballs, which is found to the right (north) of the trailhead to Turtle just after the gate on the driveway/paved access road. There are a few good problems on Meatballs but most of them are high over rocks and could use a toprope. Split Rock's main face has probably been climbed since the 1950s or 60s and it's no wonder why. The (mostly) solid, well-featured highball slab face is a perfect toprope for beginners or an exciting solo for an experienced boulderer. The steeper Turtle Rock was overlooked until two local brothers/climbing partners, Gary and Russ Bobzien, came along in the late 1970s and cleaned and climbed its more challenging faces. They established some of the most picturesque boulder problems in the Bay Area. Now you can climb the never-ending traverse or the multitude of short or high, easy to moderate problems, then sit down and enjoy some of the best views of the Bay.

Split Rock has great views of the East Bay and one of the best highball boulder slabs in the book. The main face that you see from the road is a classic 5.6R up the easiest center crack called Split Slab. The slightly harder faces and cracks to the left and right are also excellent. Stemming up (or down) the chimney is an excellent old

Valentine Cullen on Split Slab (5.6R).

school highball that goes at 5.6R. Split Rock has easy access and various cracks and small trees on top for teaching and learning to place gear, setting up safe topropes, and even making short leads.

About the rock

Ring Mountain's exotic serpentine boulders are full of rare minerals. The stone is extremely smooth and polished and usually solid. As always, be careful of the occasional loose hold, especially when you're high. The VB-V1's on Split Rock's 30-foot tall main face are a fun and worthy toprope challenge for a beginner or a thrilling highball for an expert. Turtle Rock has mostly the opposite, shorter and steeper V0-V5s and has so

Number of problems by difficulty

VB	V0	V1	V2	V3	V4	V5	V6	V7	V8	V9	V10	≥V11
7	10	3	2	1	1	1	1	0	0	0	0	0

many handholds on its short overhanging faces combined with flat landings it makes a perfect outdoor gym. It's no wonder why locals have made up so many eliminate problems over the years.

When to climb

All year. The boulders sit in grassy fields on top of a hill with few trees and are exposed to the sun + elements all day. Split gets shade on its main face in the morning and sun in the afternoon. Turtle's main face gets sun in the morning and shade in the afternoon. Because the hilltop is so exposed it would be wise to bring sunscreen on a hot day and extra layers of clothes in case it's windy. Summer can be a bit warm and sunny but still good, with a cool sea breeze that flows over Mt. Tam and the refreshing fog over the Bay. Winter can be windy and cold sometimes but the solid rock dries amazingly fast, which makes it a great place to squeeze in a quicky during a break from a storm. Spring and fall are usually perfect.

Driving Directions

From north of San Francisco, about six miles north of the Golden Gate Bridge on US-101 in Corte Madera take the Paradise Dr. exit. Follow Paradise Dr. east for about three miles to a right turn onto the short but steep Taylor Rd. Continue to the end of Taylor Rd. and find a legal place to park that is not blocking any of the driveways.

Approach

Split Rock is visible to the south of the parking area a nice five-minute stroll from the car. The trail to Turtle starts on the paved driveway/access road on the right side of the end of Taylor Rd. Follow the paved driveway/access road uphill, through a gate and up another short hill to a right turn onto a dirt road. Take the dirt road to the right and as it crests the hill Turtle Rock will be visible to the west. Total hiking time to Turtle Rock is about 5 to 10 minutes.

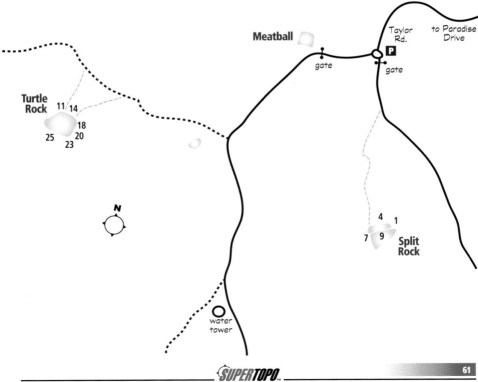

Split Rock

Split Rock can be seen from the trailhead near the parking at the end of Taylor Rd. Most of the highball climbs on Split Rock can be toproped with gear and long slings from the cracks and trees on the easily accessible top. The center of the main face is a classic highball 5.6R called Split Slab.

❏ **1. 5.8R★★★**
Highball crack/corner over rocky landing.

❏ **2. V0R★★** Arête.

❏ **3. 5.8R★★** Start left of center, go up vertical to slabby highball face.

❏ **4. Split Slab 5.6R★★★★** Center of high steep slab face with zig zagging splitter crack.

❏ **5. V0R★★★** Smooth crack/face.

❏ **6. V0+R/X★★** Highball bulgy prow.

❏ **7. The Split 5.6R★★** Chimney. Start anywhere inside the split and stem your way up.

❏ **8. West Split V1R/X★★** Start just inside the split on the left (west) side. **V4R/X Variation**: Start in the far back left (west) side of the split. Go up high vertical face.

❏ **9. East Split 5.8R/X★★** Start in the far back right (east) side of the split. Go up.

❏ **10. Split Rock Traverse V2★★★** Traverse the entire main face either from the right start on The Split (#7) and traverse to the left into #1 to finish or from #1 to the right into #7 to finish. **V4 Variation:** Start in the far back left (west) side of the split same as the V4R/X variation of #8 and traverse left past a hard face climbing section and past the starting holds of West Split (#8) to the left out of the split into the V2 start.

Turtle Rock

GPS: 37.911183, -122.491433 Problems listed from right to left:

❏ **11. Turtle Rock Traverse V5★★★★** Traverse the center of the steep face in either direction, staying below the lip. Mega classic pumpfest. Many variations: V4 Use the top lip across problems #12-18. V6 if you stay low and link into and across #16 in either direction. V8 if you stay low through the entire traverse.

❏ **12. V0-★★** Stand start on the right side of the rock scar and follow a thin seam to top. V0+ Stand start on the left side of the rock scar. Sit start is V1.

❏ **13.** V0★★ Stand start and make moves into the big under-cling, then top out straight up. **V1 Variation:** Sit start on low in-cut jug horn.

❏ **14. The Lieback** V0-★★★ Stand start right hand lieback rail. **V1 Variation:** Sit start on naturally sculpted in-cut edges and huge footholds at the base of the rock.

❏ **15.** V0★★ Stand start on wide horizontal rail and make moves up to and past a jug flake. **V1 Variation:** Sit start same as #14 then angle up left into jug flake and top out.

❏ **16.** V4★★ Sit start same as #14 then traverse low and left using powerful, side-pulls and gastons combined with good body english to stay below the wide horizontal rail on #15 and make it into #17 to finish. Many eliminates can be done on this well-featured section of wall.

❏ **17.** V1★★ Sit start on good flat edges, then go up right into the jug flake on #15 and top out. **V0 Variation:** Same sit start, then angle up left into #18.

❏ **18.** 5.6★ Stand start right bulge.
5.7 Stand start left bulge

❏ **19.** 5.8★★ Crack/Face.

❏ **20.** V0+★★★ Stand start steep jugs into highball topout. **V1** Sit start.

❏ **21.** V0★★★ Pull over right side of roof with hueco into highball finish.

❏ **22.** V0+★★★ Face left of roof. Make one move into a big hueco to start. Highball.

❏ **23. Green Face** V2★★★ Start on big foot hold and go up highball green face.

❏ **24. Gold Face** V1★★★ Just right of ledge go straight up from gold patch into highball topout.

❏ **25.** V0-★★ Stand start in center of sloper ledge and mantle onto it, then top out straight over.

Turtle Rock with Mt. Tam in the distance.

Mount Tamalpais

Problems: **100**

Rock: **Volcanic**

Difficulty: **VB-V7**

Mount Tamalpais State Park in Marin County has some of the best views of the San Francisco Bay Area I have ever seen and a lot of them are right from the seat of your car. Mt Tam is the birthplace of mountain biking with many steep trails for biking or hiking all over the mountain. Local climbers know Mt Tam as a good place to find some easy to moderate top ropes on fairly solid volcanic stone with good cracks, pockets and jugs. There has also been a slow development of bouldering going on but never more than some spread out problems of varied styles until the last few years when a few inspired local started discovering some hidden gems. The mountain now sports about 100 problems with legit access and most are on well maintained park trails or along the roadside.

Driving Directions/Approach

On US-101/CA-1 north of San Francisco, about 3.5 miles north of the Golden Gate Bridge, take the exit for CA-1 (Shoreline Highway.) North/Stinson Beach. Keep following the signs for CA-1 North/Stinson Beach. About three miles from US-101 turn right onto the Panoramic Hwy. and follow the signs to Mount Tamalpais State Park. The Intuition Boulders will be the first you come to heading up the mountain.

The Intuition Boulders (aka East Bootjack Boulders): About 7.5 miles from US-101 (or about 3.5 miles from the four-way intersection) a large pullout will be on the left side of the road, either park there or continue up the road to the Bootjack Picnic Area about a half mile away and turn around, then come back and park at the smaller pullout just before the tight corner directly below the trail uphill to the boulders. Three to five-minute hike. (5-10 problems V1 to V5/6 - classics= Intuition V5 and its variation Instinct V5/6)

Kenny Ariza on his classic Procrastination (V7) at the Lakeview boulders

East Peak Areas Directions - drive uphill about 1 mile past Intuition (or about 8.5 miles from US-101 or about 4.5 from the four-way intersection) to the intersection at the Ranger Station and turn right onto Pan Toll Rd. After about another mile you will come to the intersection at Rock Springs. Turn right onto East Ridgecrest and drive less than a mile to The Camel Pie Boulder in a large dirt parking lot on the right side of the road or continue on to the areas below;

The Bay View Boulder (on the right) and The Eastern Bloc (on the left uphill in the tress): 0.9 miles east of Rock Springs on East Ridgecrest park on top of Bay View Boulder. (15 problems V0 to V6 - classics= ATF Traverse V6 and Snake Practice V4 low sit)

The Lakeview Boulders: off Lakeview Trail before the East Peak on the north side of East Ridgecrest (30-40 problems VB to V7 - classic= Procrastinator V7 sit roof to face)

The East Peak Boulders: at the end of East Ridgecrest, 2.9 miles from the intersection at Rock Springs around the popular East Peak lookout tower (10-20 problems VB to V4)

Marin Headlands

Problems: **10**

Rock: **Chert**

Difficulty: **VB-V4**

In the hills on the north side of the Golden Gate Bridge, overlooking the mouth of the Bay and the breathtaking Pacific Coast are a few good problems on a big chert boulder known as Genocide Rock. A couple tweaky, slabby traverses, a couple short, steep sit starts, and a few highball face climbs can be found on this huge multi-angled boulder. The rock quality is good but not perfect so if you need to, a toprope can be set up for the highballs using gear, slings and old hangerless bolts. On a clear day the popular Conzelman Rd. that leads to the boulder from Hwy. 101 is lined with tourists snapping photos of the awesome views.

Classics: **Headstrong V3** or **Headstrong Traverse V4** (west face) and the **Genocide Traverse V2** or V4 sit (northeast face).

Rodeo Beach at the Marin Headlands.
Photo by Chris McNamara.

Driving Directions/Approach

From US-101 on the north side of the Golden Gate Bridge take the Marin Headlands Golden Gate Recreation Area exit. Drive 1.2 miles on Conzelman Rd. to the intersection with McCullough Rd. and park in any of the turnouts around the intersection. Hike up the steep hill to the northeast for about three to five minutes to the obvious big chert boulder.

Squaw Rock

Problems: 75-100

Rock: Schist/Greenstone

Difficulty: VB-V6, mostly V0-V4

Marcos Nunez high over the Russian River on Cracker (V0R/X).

Traffic rushes by on Highway 101 as the Russian River rushes by the giant Squaw Rock in laid back Mendocino County. About 75 good boulder problems on polished stone are spread around four different areas. The main area known as The Brave Boulders is divided in two by the river and is found to the south on Hwy. 101 (downstream) from the huge cliff on Squaw Rock. Unfortunately, the highest concentration of boulder problems (about 30) is across the river from the highway and in winter it is impossible to get to them safely across the white water rapids. In summer and especially late summer the river is usually low enough to find a good place to cross on seasonally changing sandbars. There are also a few good sport climbs across the river at The Brave Boulders and on Squaw Rock. The two bolt 5.10 across the river called Braveheart is a great highball V0R/X. On the highway side of The Brave Boulders there are about 20 good problems from V0-V6. There are about 15 more good problems from V0-V4 below the highway across from the base of Squaw Rock. These boulders are named The Squaw Boulders and in winter most of them are underwater with the exception of a couple roadside classics. The final area called the Untamed Rocks has uncertain access and parking is a problem so I will just give a brief description: Untamed Rocks are just north of Squaw Rock off the side of 101 and have about 10 problems from V0-V5 and a few sport/trad climbs from 5.10-5.12.

Classics: **Cracker V0R/X** (Squaw Boulders), **Trickery V6** and **Flowmaster V1** (Brave Boulders, below US-101), **Powerslave V6** and **Braverheart V0R/X** (Brave Boulders, across river from US-101).

The Brave Boulders Directions/Approach

Park in the turnouts on the west (river) side of US-101 about seven miles north of CA-128 west in Cloverdale and about six miles south of CA-175 east in Hopland. Follow trails down to the boulders along the river's edge. In late summer the river is usually low enough to cross to the main boulders on the other side. Good luck finding the seasonally changing sandbars to cross on.

The Squaw Boulders Directions/Approach

Park on the west (river) side of US-101 in a long turnout across the river from the base of the huge cliff on Squaw Rock about 7.4 miles north of CA-128 west in Cloverdale and about 5.8 miles south of CA-175 east in Hopland. The boulders are just below the highway along the bank of the river.

Mossy Rock

Number of problems: 15-25

Rock: Volcanic

Difficulty: VB-V5

The pockety highball face of Mossy Rock has been climbed since at least the early 1980s as a short toprope or highball boulder problem but not until the recent popularity of bouldering has its other faces gotten much attention. Sitting on the side of the popular Mossy Rock Trail, a popular hiking/mountain biking trail in the hills outside of Angwin, is Napa County's exclusive bouldering area. This is also a great place to get out and enjoy a beautiful forest on foot, on bike, and on rock. The pocketed volcanic stone is similar to that of the nearby sport crags Bubble Rock and The Far Side on Mt. Saint Helena. There are about 10 to 15 good boulder problems from 5.6–V5 at Mossy and about 5 to 10 more partially developed boulders from 5.6-V5 further up the trails at the Angwish Boulders.

Classics: **Footloose V2r** (center face), **No Brain No Pain V3** (stand start, left face), **No Pain No Gain V4** (sit start to left face), **Dirty Dancin V0** (face right of prow), **Mossy Rock Traverse V4,** and the **Angwish Traverse V5.**

Driving Directions/Approach

From CA-29 or Silverado Trail just north of the town of Saint Helena in Napa County take Howell Mountain Rd. east past Deer Park to Angwin. As you enter town take a right on Cold Springs Rd. (just before the Pacific Union College (which has a climbing wall). Follow it to Las Posadas Rd., then drive about a mile past some vineyards to a sharp right hand turn. Park on the left in the obvious large dirt pullout. Follow the middle of the three trails straight for about a minute (or two) to an opening in the fence (tight squeeze with a pad), then continue straight ahead for about another minute (or

Professor Floyd on Mossy Rock.

two) to a four-way intersection with a dirt road.

Continue straight through the intersection and in another couple minutes you will be at another intersection. Follow the trail to the right. After about 5 to 10 more minutes of good flat single track you'll see Mossy Rock on the left side. Total hiking time from the car to Mossy Rock is about 10 to 15 minutes.

Sugarloaf Ridge State Park

Problems: 50

Rock: **Volcanic and Schist**

Difficulty: **VB-V7, mostly V1-V4**

Sugarloaf has been called The North Bay's Castle Rock. Although it's nowhere near as good in quality or quantity of bouldering to its South Bay compadre, the park does have a similar vibe. Well-maintained trails embraced by redwood forests lead you to almost every boulder in the park. The boulders are a mix of three different types of rock. The first type is a solid pockety volcanic and is the most common. Second is a softer knobby volcanic that is found at the Lower Canyon Trail Boulders. Third and least common in the park is schist. The boulder problems are on varied angles from short and steep to high and slabby.

Val and Holly Hike Canyon Trail.

About the rock

A lot of good, short, steep problems and a few good highballs on a variety of different feeling stone. The boulders above the waterfall off the sides of Canyon Trail have the most solid rock and the highest concentration of problems, with the exception of the few good problems on the tasty Biscuit Boulder. Arêtes, pockets, knobs, and an occasional soft, leaf and twig-covered landing give the often overlooked boulders a surprisingly fun and unforgettable feel.

When to climb

Generally it's good all year but spring, summer and fall are consistently the best. Winter can be a bit cold and damp under the shady canopy of trees that covers most of the boulders but that shade also keeps the boulders cool in the heat of summer. A lot of the Lower Canyon Trail Boulders are wet all winter, with the exception of the excellent Neptune Boulder, and a few of the problems on the backside of the Asteroid Boulders which are usually dry after a few days of sun.

Number of problems by difficulty

VB	V0	V1	V2	V3	V4	V5	V6	V7	V8	V9	V10	≥V11
1	5	11	9	8	6	2	2	2	0	0	0	0

Driving Directions

Less than a mile west of Kenwood, "the pillow fighting capitol of the world," on CA-12 and 11.0 miles east of the US101/ CA-12 intersection in Santa Rosa is Adobe Canyon Rd. Coming from Santa Rosa, it's 6.0 miles east of the Calistoga Rd./CA-12 intersection on CA-12 to the left turn for Adobe Canyon Rd. Follow Adobe Canyon Rd. for 2.0 miles to the entrance of Sugarloaf Ridge State Park. All of the bouldering areas are within the park boundaries but only one (luckily the smallest one), The Sunrise Boulders, are inside the fee area beyond the campground at the top of the road. Campground parking is $6 and a campsite is $15. There is NO parking from 8pm-6am. There are NO dogs allowed on any trails in the park and dogs must be on a leash when out of any vehicle—this is enforced, believe me. Most of the boulder problems are found at the Canyon Trail Boulders above the waterfall on upper Canyon Trail. Most of the hard problems are found on the boulders in the creek below lower Canyon Trail on the Asteroid Boulders but are usually wet all winter. GPS: Upper Canyon Trail Parking Lot: 38.438333, -122.51875

Vanessa Wight spots Valentine Cullen on Pyramid Arête (V1).

Chad Ramos on Hate (V1).

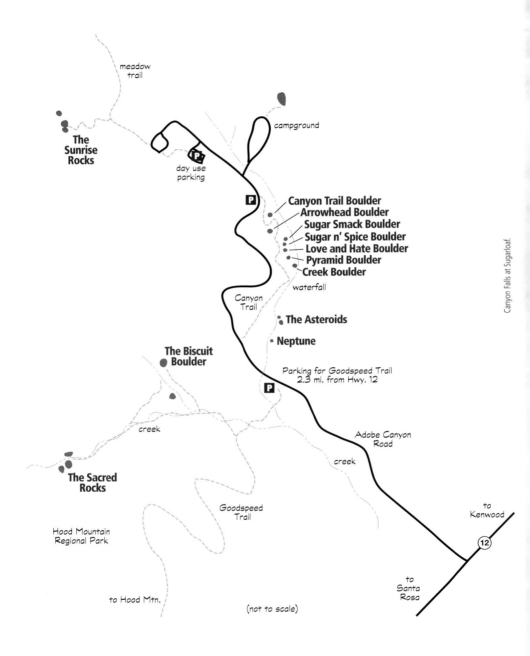

meadow
trail

campground

**The
Sunrise
Rocks**

day use
parking

Canyon Trail Boulder
Arrowhead Boulder
Sugar Smack Boulder
Sugar n' Spice Boulder
Love and Hate Boulder
Pyramid Boulder
Creek Boulder

waterfall

Canyon
Trail

The Asteroids

Neptune

**The Biscuit
Boulder**

Parking for Goodspeed Trail
2.3 mi. from Hwy. 12

creek

Adobe Canyon
Road

creek

**The Sacred
Rocks**

to
Kenwood

Goodspeed
Trail

Hood Mountain
Regional Park

(12)

to
Santa
Rosa

to Hood Mtn.

(not to scale)

Canyon Falls at Sugarloaf.

Sacred Rocks and Biscuit Boulder

From the first parking lot, Goodspeed Trail goes for 3.5 miles uphill to the excellent views at Gunsight Rock and the peak of Hood Mountain. There are 15 problems within about one mile of the parking lot I will tell about but not give maps or pics for. This is because most of them are far from established trails and have less-traveled rock, which can mean loose, dirty holds and bad landings. The enjoyable Biscuit Boulder is the exception.

Biscuit Boulder Directions

To find the tasty Biscuit Boulder follow Goodspeed Trail from the parking lot over the two footbridges, then hang a right after the second bridge onto a much smaller deer trail that follows the creek. Follow the creek upstream until you see the first smaller (seasonal) stream coming in from the right. Follow this small stream uphill past a little heart-shaped boulder with a V1 on it called Heartbreaker. The Biscuit Boulder will be just uphill on the right.

Biscuit Boulder

❏ **1. The Biscuit Traverse** V3★★ Traverse low horizontal crack/rail from left to right (uphill). V3R Into Butterscotch (#4).

❏ **2. Buttercup** V4★★★ Sit start on left side of boulder on horizontal crack and go up the steep face past the buttercup shaped handhold to the jug and either drop or top.

❏ **3. Buttercup Dyno** V5★★ Dyno to the top jug, skipping the buttercup hold.

❏ **4. Butterscotch** V2R★★ Climb up face on right with horizontals and pass a natural thread pocket before the highball topout.

❏ **5. Brown Sugar** V2★★ Upper Traverse. **V3R Variaiton:** Climb into into #4.

Sacred Rocks Directions

Follow Goodspeed Trail over the two footbridges the same as the directions to the Biscuit Boulder and continue following the main creek upstream passing the small (seasonal) stream on the right that is the turn for the Biscuit Boulder. After following the main creek upstream for about 20 minutes from the parking lot, the Sacred Rocks will come into view. They cannot be missed because they hang over the creek, forming an arch.

Sacred Rocks

❏ **6. The Sacred Traverse** V3 or V4★★ Traverse the base of the big boulder in either direction; 50 foot long. Low V4 High V3.

❏ **7. The Sugar Traverse** V5★★ Do The Sacred Traverse low from left to right into #8 to finish. **Sugarhigh V4:** Stay high on the traverse.

❏ **8. Call of the Wild** V3★★ Stand start on the right side of the overhanging main face of the big boulder and pull over bulge onto the slab to the right to topout.

❏ **9. Enchanted** V4★★ Traverse the smaller boulder upstream from the main problems. Sit start on the left arête, then traverse the lip to the right. Arête by itself is V2.

❏ **10. White Fang** V6★★ Sit start right of #9 and crank up past the fang to topout on slab. Left or right variations are both V6.

The Sunrise Boulders Directions

These boulders get their name from the early morning sunlight that they receive all year. To get to The Sunrise Boulders you will either have to pay the day use fee of $6 or get a campsite ($15) and park inside the fee area or park outside at the Upper Canyon Trail parking lot and walk in for free. Since you will have to hike close to a mile from the day use parking lot inside the fee area anyway, the extra 1/4 mile from the free parking area at Upper Canyon Trail is maybe not such a bad idea if you want to save the six bucks. Once inside the fee area at the day use parking lot, take Meadow Trail over a short hill to the next parking lot, then still following Meadow Trail go straight across the meadow to where the trail makes a right hand turn. Take a left off of Meadow Trail and follow faint deer trails up a small creek for about five minutes to The Sunrise Boulders. Total hiking time from Day Use Parking is about 10 to 15 minutes.

The Sunrise Boulders

❏ **11. Sundial** V2★★ Sit start in the center of the main face of the big boulder and go up.

❏ **12.** V1★ Stand start on the left (uphill) side of the main face of the big boulder.

❏ **13. The Sunrise Traverse** V3★ Stand start on the right corner of the main face of the big boulder and traverse up and left.

❏ **14. Matchbox** V4★ Short hard traverse on the backside of the big main boulder from inside a tight corridor to the right, then around arête and up slab.

❏ **15.** V1★★ Stand start in center of steep face, then pull over bulge on smaller boulder uphill from the big boulder.

Canyon Trail Boulders

The Canyon Trail Boulders have the highest concentration of problems and are also the most easily accesible in the park. This collection of volcanic boulders are all found off the popular Canyon Trail and have a wide variety of challenges from V0-V7. GPS of intersection of trails above waterfall: 38.438833, -122.52175

Canyon Trail Boulder

❏ **16. Trailblazer** V2★★ Stand start face left of arête that faces trail. The sit start is V3.

❏ **17. Trailblazer Arête** V1★★ Stand start short bulging arête. The sit start is V2.

❏ **18. Short 'n' Sweet** V0★★ Face right of arête. Good landing, good fun.

❏ **19. Fishy Climb** 5.4★ Short mossy face.

❏ **20.** V1★ Short steep sit start on a small boulder opposite #16–#19.

Arrowhead Boulder

❏ **21. Arrow Arête** V2★ Left Arête. Stand start. Bad landing.

❏ **22. Arrowhead** V3★ Sit start in the center of the vertical main face of the Arrowhead Boulder over a bad rocky landing.

❏ **23. Flaming Arrow** V1★★ Sit start down and right of the main Arrowhead Face.

❏ **24. Arrowhead Traverse** V4★ Sit start #23, then traverse left, over rocks (staying low) across #22 into #21 to finish. Bad landing.

❏ **25.** V1★ Traverse left into V0 face in corner on the small boulder across the talus field from the Arrowhead Boulder.

Sugar n Spice Boulder

❏ **26. Suga Mama** V1★★ Stand start right hand arête. V2 Sit start on jug shelf.

❏ **27. Suga Daddy** V3★★ Sit or stand start steep highball slab face right of arête.

❏ **28. Spice** V0R★ Stand start steep highball slab crack right of #27.

Sugar Smack Boulder

❏ **29.** V1★ Stand start on right hand crimp and left hand lie-back edge and go up and left into #30 to finish. **V3 Variation:** Direct straight up over top.

❏ **30. Sugar Smack** V3★★ Sit start on crimper edges and go straight up past sloper rail into high slab/arête finish. The stand start is V2.

❏ **31. V2★★** Stand start with left hand on a flat, dark brown-colored (rock scar) hold and traverse slab up and left along small footholds to finish on the big ledge on the left.

❏ **32. Finga Tingla** V3★★ Stand start #31 and traverse left past the crux up into direct left hand lieback face finish.

Love n Hate Boulder

❏ **33. Love** V0★★ Stand start on right hand diagonal arête. Traverse up and left along the bomber arête to the same topout as #19. Low sit start is V1.

❏ **34. Hate** V1★★ Stand or sit and climb left arête. Detached boulder at base is on for feet.

❏ **35. Love 'n' Hate** V4★★ Sit start #33, then traverse left across a hard scrunchy crux, staying below (off) right arête (#33) into left arête (#34). Detached boulder at base is off for feet. If used it's V3.

Pyramid Boulder

❏ **36. Pyramid Arête (A.K.A. Triangle Arête)** V0-V2★★ Short steep arête. V0: Stand start on jug lip of arête. V1: Low stand start on sloper rail. V2: Sit start on the lowest part of arête, down and left of V1 start.

❏ **37. Pyramid Power** V2★★ Sit start with left hand lie-back and small right hand sloper edge and bust a move up to flat jug. V0 Stand start on flat jug. V5 Same sit start, then go left into #36 avoiding the flat jug.

❏ **38. Pyramid Traverse** V3★★ Sit start on far right side of boulder and traverse along slopey diagonal lip up and left into the same topout as #37.

❏ **39. V1★** Sit start on big flat ledge and make moves up and right, then pull onto the slab to finish. Either step off or top out via 5.6r slab.

Creek Boulder (Downhill from Pyramid)

❏ **40. V3★★** Sit or low stand start into steep slab face on left side of boulder.

❏ **41. Creek Face** V4★★ Sit start in center of steep slab face with hands on big slopey ledge. V0 Stand start with feet on big ledge.

❏ **42. Lockwood** V3★★ Sit start right face. Crimpy gastons and side-pulls up steep slab.

The Asteroid Boulders/Neptune Boulders

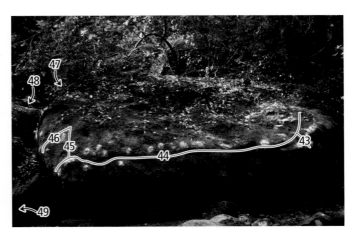

These boulders are the softest (most friable) rock in the park and also some of the softest in the whole guide. Be careful not to climb on them too soon after a rain. Also be careful not to over brush or wire brush them. Problems #44, #45, and #46 are often wet from fall to spring (about November to June) from the nearby creek. Give the boulders about three to five days after a rain to dry, depending on how much it rained and how sunny it got after the rain. Quite often the rocks in this shady canyon will not dry out enough to climb all winter. UPDATE 2010; unfortuantely a huge tree fell down against #44, 45 and 46 a few winters ago making them unclimbable :(and the moss and leaves and needles is always a factor so bring a brush and be prepared to use it.

The Asteroid Boulders

❑ **43. Asteroid** V0★★ Low stand start on a knobby horizontal edge, then make moves up to big knobs and top out. Far right side of Asteroid boulder. Short but hard. Meteor V1 Sit start down and left.

❑ **44. Milky Way Traverse** V7★★ Sit start on two crimpy knobs. Make a move up to a sloper, then traverse right along the bulgy overhang past more slopers and knobs into #43 to finish. V6 Stand start on sloper.

❑ **45. Space Monkey** V4★★ Same sit start as #44 past sloper, then go up past pocket into slopey topout. V2 Stand start on sloper.

❑ **46.** V2★★ Stand start left of #44 and #45 on a flat right hand knob/edge and a left hand slopey edge and go straight up over

the top. Far left side of boulder.

❑ **47. Orbit** V5★★ Low stand start in the center of short overhanging face on small edges that are an inch apart. Make one hard move up to good knobs on the lip, then pull over onto the slab to topout. V1 Stand start on the lip.

❑ **48. Uranus** V3★ Sit start on a left hand lie-back/right hand gaston edge and go up and right into bulgy topout.

❑ **49. The Fifth Element** V5★★ Sit start at the water's edge on a short arête with a low right hand pocket and a small left hand pocket, then traverse up and left into the V1 arête finish. **The Fourt Element V4**: Stand start to Fifth Element.

Neptune Boulder

❑ **50. Neptune** V6★★★ Start in hueco (hole) and go up intothe slopey left arête. **Neptune Direct V7**: same start but go straight up the overhanging face right of the arête. V5 Stand start on lip.

Putah Creek (Purgatory)

Problems: **30**

Rock: **Basalt**

Difficulty: **VB-V9, mostly V0-V6**

Purgatory is said to be an ominous place between heaven and hell and it is also a fitting nickname for these dark, foreboding rocks in the middle of nowhere. Back in the late 1990s when I was a regular here I heard it called Purgatory by a few locals and it kind of stuck (not to be confused with the Purtgatory Boulders in Northern Nevada, obviously). Most people simply call it Putah. If you don't watch your p's and q's, Putah can sound a lot like a naughty word in Spanish—so get it straight. Whatever you want to call it, it's one of the best roadside bouldering playgrounds in the North Bay. The Purgatory Boulder has a few of the best problems in the guide, all on its clean, overhanging, highball main face. The frigid water of Putah Creek flows silent and deep alongside these big boulders after squirting out of the bottom of Lake Berryessa through the "glory hole" at the base of Monticello Dam a few miles upstream. Fishing and swimming are also possible right next to the rocks and up the road at Lake Berryessa. Of course lounging on the beach and bird watching are always options as well. Occasionally you will catch a glimpse of a river otter fishing and lounging with you. If you're lucky you'll get to see the swallows that nest on the creek side of the Purgatory Boulder. They only stop for about a month or two every year along their migratory journeys. If you're really lucky you'll get to see them all fly out of their nests around sunset and do laps over the creek in a routine that can leave a tired boulderer in a sort of delirious trance.

Sean Brady warms up on Heavy Metal (V0).

About the rock

This is the same basalt as the nearby Vacaville Boulders. It's usually solid, but look out for some loose holds, especially on the less popular rocks. There are two main boulders at Putah with the problems generally being easier on the taller one and harder on the steeper, shorter one. The boulders have the telltale octagonal column shapes seen on other basalt, but at Putah they are much smaller and turned in a variety of ways. Usually they are pointing up and out so you get to grab the big square cut edges around the sides. On overhanging rock (which most of the problems are on) this makes for some fantastic gymnastics.

Number of problems by difficulty

VB	V0	V1	V2	V3	V4	V5	V6	V7	V8	V9	V10	≥V11
7	5	6	3	1	2	1	2	1	1	1	0	0

When to climb

All year is usually all good. The summer can be hot and Monticello Dam on Lake Berryessa just a few miles upstream releases water from the lake occasionally. How much and how often changes seasonally. When the dam is releasing extra water the creek will rise up around some of the problems. Only a few of the problems usually get flooded for long; the rest might get muddy landings as a result. The muddy landings can stay wet for months during the winter, so rather than playing leap frog hopping from pad to pad to keep your shoes dry, just bring a tarp.

Driving Directions

From most Bay Area locations take I-80 east to Vacaville, then follow I-505 north to Winters. From Winters take CA-128 west toward Lake Berryessa. About 7.7 miles west of I-505 in Winters, park in a dirt tunout on the west (creek) side of CA-128.

Coming from the North Bay and Napa area it is possibly better to follow the previous directions unless you enjoy driving on windy backroads.

From the north side of Napa take Trancas St. from CA-29 to CA-121/Monticello Rd. From the south side of Napa take Soscol from CA-12 to CA-121/Silverado Trail then follow it to CA-121/Monticello Rd. Follow CA-121/Monticello Rd. to CA-128 then turn right onto CA-128 east toward Winters. At Monticello Dam on the east side of Lake Berryessa, set your odometer at the viewpoint parking lot and go 3.2 miles farther east on CA-128 to the parking on the west (creek) side of CA-128.

From north of Napa, about three miles south of Saint Helena on CA-29, turn onto CA-128 east to Lake Berryessa and Winters. Drive 16 miles to the viewpoint at Monticello Dam. Set your odometer at the viewpoint parking lot and go 3.2 miles farther east on CA-128 to the parking on the west (creek) side of CA-128. Parking Lot GPS: 38.517383, -122.05605

Approach

Follow a good but sometimes overgrown trail a short way to the boulders in the shady forest between the highway and the creek.

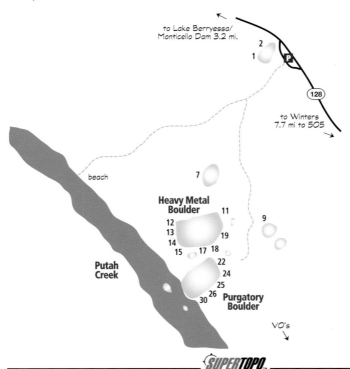

to Lake Berryessa/
Monticello Dam 3.2 mi.

2
1
P

128

to Winters
7.7 mi to 505

beach

7

Heavy Metal Boulder   11

12   9
13
14   19
15   17 18

Putah
Creek

22
24
25
30 26 **Purgatory Boulder**

VO's

Roadside Boulder

❏ **1. V0★★** Stand start with feet on big ledge and hands on big flat rail or a move lower on left hand side-pull jug and right hand sloper. Make moves past jug rail and up right arête.

❏ **2. Roadside Traverse V6/7★★** Same start as #1 (Stand start with feet on big ledge and hands on big flat rail or a move lower on left hand side-pull jug and right hand sloper.) Make moves up and left past the side-pull jug rail into the upper line of holds and traverse left (just below the lip of the boulder) to finish on the far left side. **V8/V9 Low Variation:** Stay low across the lower line of edges to the same finish on the far left.

❏ **3. V1★★** Start same as #1 and #2 with feet on big ledge and do the same start moves as the Roadside Traverse V6/7 up and left then top out.

❏ **4. V1★★★** Stand start in center of face on left hand pocket or left hand side-pull and go up. The sit start is V3.

❏ **5. V2★★** Stand start on good crimpers and go up left face. V3 Sit start.

The Weasel Boulder

❏ **6. Chickadee 5.6★★** Center of slab face.

❏ **7. The Weasel 5.6★★** Stand start arête/corner.

❏ **8. Nut Face 5.7★★** Stand start face left of crack. The short diagonal crack is 5.4.

The Mud-Hole Boulder

❏ **9. Mud-hole V1★★** Left sit start.

❏ **10. Pumpkin Eater V1★★** Center sit start.

Heavy Metal Boulder

❏ **11. Crooked Cross Traverse V5★★** Sit start on right side. Short traverse left along horizontal crack. **V2 Variation:** Stay high using all holds.

❏ **12. 5.6R★★** Stand start on big blocky jugs and go up over bulge to finish on highball slab left of #13 and #14.

❏ **13. 5.8R★★** Stand start on good in-cut/square-cut edges and go up vertical face into highball slab.

❏ **14. 5.8R★★** Stand start on in-cut edges just right of #13 and go up vertical face into highball slab.

❏ **15. V0R or V1★★** Stand start on microwave-size blocks on arête. Go up right side of arête V1 or go up left side V0R. **V2 Variation:** Start on #16.

❏ **16. V2★★** Sit start off rock and go up center of face. **V5 Low sit start:** under mini roof just right of arête on left hand in-cut edge and right hand on small flat crimper edge and pull out direct over roof into the V2 start.

❏ **17. Heavy Metal V0★★★** Stand start off rock on a head high in-cut right hand gaston and left hand crimp. Go up. **V1 sit start:** on flat two hand edge and go up and right into V0 stand start to finish.

❏ **18. Heavy Metal Traverse V4★★★** Usually done right to left from a wide, head high jug rail just left of the 4th class down climb (#19) on the north side of the boulder. Good in either direction or for doing laps. Long technical power endurance traverse. Arm-burning hell fire.

❏ **19. 4th Class** Down climb.

Purgatory Boulder

The base of all the problems on the Purgatory Boulder (#20-#30) is just below the high water mark. Occasionally during the rainy season these problems will be underwater for a few days at a time. Most often in winter the landings will be muddy and require a tarp to keep your shoes and pad dry.

❏ **20. V2**★★ Arête. Sit start on a low sharp right hand edge and left hand side-pull. Go up and left then pull around right to finish. **V1 Variation**: Same sit start as #20, then move right onto slab.

❏ **21. Chocolat V6**★★ Sit start arête (#20) then traverse up and left past #22 and #23 into the final crux of #24 to finish.

❏ **22. Hell Awaits V3 or V4**★★★★ **V3 High stand start:** With right hand horn or just lower on good crimper edges, go up center of steep highball face. **V4 Low stand start:** On right hand sloper pinch and left hand sloper edge, fire a few moves into the high stand start. High start FA: Chris Summit, 1993.

❏ **23. Hellspawn V7 or V8**★★★★ Squat start with both arms spread apart on matching side-pull rails and throw a few big moves up into the V4 Low Stand Start to Hell Awaits (#22) to finish. **V8 Low sit start:** With both hands matched on the lowest left hand lie-back side-pull rail, throw one hard move out to the opposite right hand side-pull on the V7 Sit Start and do it to finish. FA: V7 by C. Summit, 1997. V8 by Charlie Barrett, 2001.

❏ **24. S.H.P. V4 or V5**★★★★ Stand start on high left hand notch pocket and right hand on small crimpy side-pull edge and go up steep slappy prow. **V5 Sit start:** From low right hand under-cling edge and sloper left hand side-pull, do a few tic tac moves up into the V4 stand start to finish. FA: Shawn Rogers, 1993.

❏ **25. Purgatory V1**★★★★ Stand start with V-slots and under-cling pinch. Bust a move up to big jug slot, then top out highball slab finish. **V2 Variation:** Sit start with either hand in blocky slot.

❏ **26. V0**★★ Same stand start as the traverse (#27) on a good left hand hold and a right hand pinch hold and make moves up to the jug shelf in the mini corner and top out the highball slab. A spotter is good.

❏ **27. Welcome to Whine Country V8**★★★★
Same stand start as #26 on a good left hand hold and a right hand pinch. Traverse right past #22–#25 to finish pulling around arête #20. A key hold broke off a few years ago, forcing the traverse to take a higher line of holds through the crux in order to maintain the same grade. Going low thru the crux past the edge that was left when the hold broke would be possibly a grade or two harder. Technical power endurance traverse. Don't cry if you slip off the onion bulb. FA: Mike Papciak, 1995.

The next three problems (#28–#30) are all at the waters edge. When the water rises the ledge at the base of the problems becomes submerged in water, making these problems inaccessible.

❏ **28. Welcome to Hell V9**★★ Same start as #29 on a flat jug shelf at the water's edge and traverse up and right past a short crux over bad landing to join the start of #27, the Welcome to Whine Country traverse. Long, pumpy technical power endurance.

❏ **29. Fishbait V0R**★★ Stand start right face. **Sleeping With the Fishes V2**: Sit start. **Fishy V4**: Sit start same as Sleeping with the Fishes then diagonal traverse up and right into #26 and top it out to finish.

❏ **30. Splash V1R**★★ Stand start and angle up and left over water. Try not to make a splash.

Sean Brady on Hellspawn, V7.

Mike Papciak at Putah Creek. Photo by Jim Thornburg.

Vacaville (Nut Tree Boulders)

Problems: **50**

Rock: **Basalt**

Difficulty: **VB-V9, mostly V0-V4**

A plethora of basalt boulders cover the peaceful grassy hills inside Vacaville Open Space. Vaca means cow in Spanish, so don't be surprised to see a lot of happy California cows grazing all around the trails and boulders. Small stone walls built around the boulders are to keep the cows from crapping and making potholes under the problems, so please do not tip the walls over (or the cows). High enough above the suburban sprawl that you can barely hear a lawn mower or a school bell, these boulders are always a nice place to hang out with great views of the Sacramento Valley and on a clear enough day, even the snow capped Sierra. Bay Area climbing legend Scott Frye did the hardest problem, Scott's Traverse V7/9. Vacaville local Aaron Rough did a lot of development along with my friend Sean Brady and I. Some of the best of our original classics were Nutcracker, Buttcracker, Stoned Dangler and Gimme My Forty Sucka. Long before all of us was the original Vacaville pioneer, Charlie Big Wall Wyatt, who was probably the first to ever boulder in the Open Space. He did the first ascents of mega-classics like Stonewall Traverse and Bloody Madness back in the late 80s/early 90s. By the late 1990s new route development slowed down and most of the good lines had been done. Only a few good hard lines were left and eventually even they would get ticked by the amazingly strong Ethan Pringle with his micro sicky Barf V7 and finally in 2004 local Justin Alarcon sent the powerful Bloodsport V7.

Eric Holt on Gimme My 40 Sucka (V1).

About the Rock

This is the same basalt as nearby Putah Creek. It's usually solid, but look out for some loose holds, especially on the less popular rocks. The boulder problems are an even mix of lowballs, highballs and pumpy traverses from V0 to V9. The handholds are good flat edges, in-cut buckets and an occasional crack. A lot of the landings are flat dirt or nice grassy fields, but quite a few have roots or rocks and require a pad or two. Most all the boulders have nice views.

Number of problems by difficulty

VB	V0	V1	V2	V3	V4	V5	V6	V7	V8	V9	V10	≥V11
2	10	7	13	4	5	2	2	3	0	1	0	0

When to Climb

All year is mostly all good. Spring and fall are usually perfect, but summertime can get hot and a lot of the boulders have little shade (you have to wait for the sun to set). Winter can have good conditions. It rains about as much here as everywhere else in Northern California but the smooth, solid, sun baked rocks dry quickly after a storm. They offer a respite from the gym in the middle of winter when a lot of the other nearby rocks are either shady and wet. During winter, the landings under the boulder problems can be wet and muddy long after the rain. A tarp can help keep your crash pad and shoes dry .

Driving Directions

West of Sacramento and east of Fairfield on I-80 in Vacaville exit onto I-505 north, then take the first exit onto Vaca Valley Pkwy. Drive for about 1.5 miles to Browns Valley Rd. From here, follow the directions to the separate areas:

Woodcrest Boulders: From the intersection of Vaca Valley Pkwy. and Browns Valley Rd. turn left onto Browns Valley Rd. and drive about one mile to a right turn onto Wrentham Dr., then take the third left off Wrentham Dr. onto Woodcrest Dr. and park on the right near the trailhead to the Open Space.

Hillcrest Boulders: From the intersection of Vaca Valley Pkwy. and Browns Valley Rd. continue on Vaca Valley Pkwy. across Browns Valley Rd. and take the second right onto Hillcrest Circle. At the end of Hillcrest Circle, when the road makes a sharp left, park near the trailhead to the Open Space.

Boxcar Woody: From the intersection of Vaca Valley Pkwy. and Browns Valley Rd. continue on Vaca Valley Pkwy. across Browns Valley Rd. to the right turn for Wrentham Dr. The Boxcar Woody is on the side of Vaca Valley Pkwy. above the retaining wall, directly across from the intersection with Wrentham Dr.

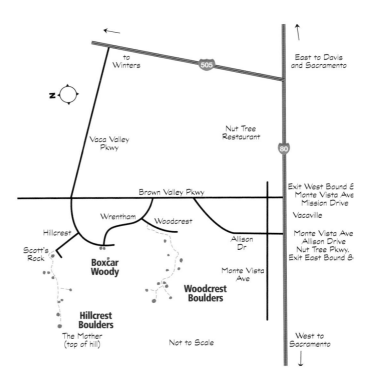

Nut Tree Boulders

The Nut Tree Boulders are divided into two main areas: Woodcrest and Hillcrest with separate parking for each and a third smaller roadside attraction, The Boxcar Boulder in between.

Boxcar Boulder

The Boxcar Boulder is a roadside classic. Overlooked at first, it became a classic after a psyched crew from Bezerkly cleaned the main face of the big boulder and turned it into their own outdoor training ground they dubbed The Boxcar Woody. GPS for parking on the corner of Wrentham and Vaca Valley Parkway: 38.388917, -121.984467

The Boxcar Woody

The Main Face of The Boxcar Boulder is known as The Boxcar Woody.

❏ **1. Boxcar Arête V0★★** Stand start. Or V1 Sit start. The short steep arête on the left side of The Boxcar Woody.

❏ **2. Boxcar Woody V2 or V3★★** V2 way: Sit start in the center of the main face above the road. Pull off the ground using a four finger in-cut V-slot tooth and go up right over chossy arête. V3 way: Go up left and top out in the center of the main face. Lots of eliminates.

❏ **3. The Boxcar Traverse V4★★** Traverse the entire Boxcar Boulder in either direction, staying below the top lip across the center of The Boxcar Woody.

❏ **4. Be V0★★** Traverse the left side of The Boxcar Boulder.

❏ **5. V2★★** Traverse the right side of The Boxcar Boulder.

The Woodcrest Boulders

The Woodcrest Boulders are home to The Stonewall Boulder, the first and still the most popular area in Vacaville. All around the main Stonewall Boulders are a variety of good easier and harder problems to play on. The Cave in the crack/corridor between the two large rocks that form The Stonewall Boulder has a couple good, steep problems with bad landings called Nutcracker V2 and Buttcracker V5. The Boulder of Bloody Madness and the Orange Boulder are both a short walk uphill from The Stonewall Boulder and offer problems from V1 to V7. Down the hill, on the trail up from the road, are a few more good boulders mingling with a bunch of bad apples. GPS Parking on Woodcrest Drive: 38.377533 -121.981

Trailside Boulders

❏ **6. RNA V1★★** Sit start on the left side of the small overhanging face.

❏ **7. DNA V2★★** Sit start matched on the low under-cling just right of #6.

❏ **8. Barf V7★** low sit start on the far right side of the overhang.

❏ **9. Cattle Drive V2★★** Start on the far right side of the large boulder and traverse left across a steep face into Cow Tipping (#10) for an exciting finish.

❏ **10. Cow Tipping V0+★★** Stand start and up over short steep mini roof.

Stonewall Boulder

GPS The Stonewall Boulder: 38.376683, -121.984583

❏ **11. Stonewall Traverse V1★★★★** Usually done right to left from a sit or stand start. Traverse good hand and foot rails on the east face of The Stonewall Boulder. It's V3 if you stay low below the main hand rail.

❏ **12. V0★★** Stand start close to the rock on the far right side of the main (east) face of The Stonewall Boulder and go up the right hand lie-back crack seam. The sit start is V1.

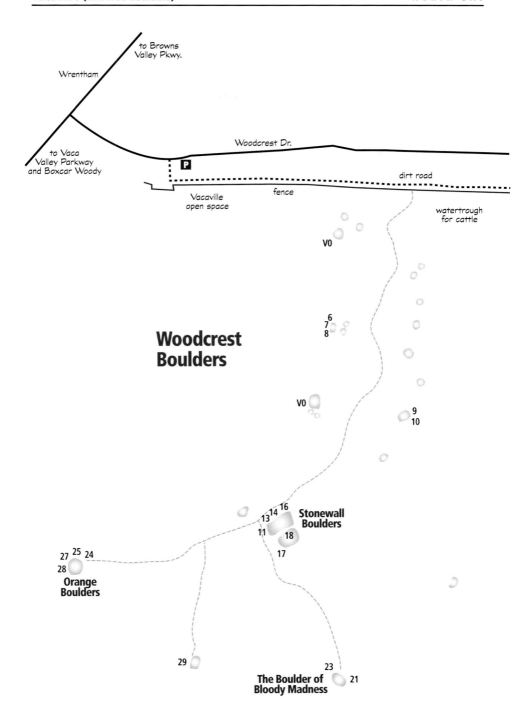

to Browns
Valley Pkwy.

Wrentham

to Vaca
Valley Parkway
and Boxcar Woody

Woodcrest Dr.

P

dirt road

Vacaville
open space

fence

watertrough
for cattle

V0

**Woodcrest
Boulders**

6
7
8

V0

9
10

13 14 16

**Stonewall
Boulders**

11

18

17

27 25 24

28

**Orange
Boulders**

29

23

**The Boulder of
Bloody Madness**   21

☐ **14. The Stonewall V0★★★** Stand start slightly overhung face. V1 Sit start on diagonal right hand edges.

☐ **15. V0★★** Low stand start on four-foot-high horizontal jug rail. Go up.

☐ **16. 5.7★★** Stand start – big edges up slabby face.

☐ **17. Suburban Hell Hole V3★★** Sit start short steep face over rocky pit.

☐ **18. Nutcracker V2★★** Sit start to zig zagging crack. Bad landing.

☐ **19. Buttcracker V5★★** Sit start in cave, go up center of steep face left of #18. Bad landing.

☐ **20. V1★** Traverse the face of the boulder just north of The Stonewall Boulder.

Boulder of Bloody Madness

☐ **21. Bloody Madness V2★★★** Stand start just left of center on steep face. V3 Sit start.

☐ **22. V1★★** Stand Start. Overhanging face to the right of #21. Sit start is V2.

☐ **23. Stoned Dangler V6★★★** Stand start on the far right side of the boulder and traverse left around the initial corner and along the steep bushy rails to finish on the jugs on the far left side of the boulder.

Orange Crush Boulder

#24-#27 usually have a wet and muddy landing in winter so bring a tarp to keep your pad dry.

☐ **24. Bloodsport V7★★** Sit start on small edges just right of the left side of the face. Do a few powerful moves on small crimper edges up into the high topout.

☐ **25. Orange Juice V2★★** Stand start on steep orange lichen covered face.

☐ **26. Orange Crush V5★★** Low stand start on good left hand edge and small right edge. Do a few powerful moves up into # 25 to finish.

❏ **27. V3★★** Low start under short steep bulge then maneuver up onto mossy slab.

❏ **28. Tree Hugger V3★★** Sit start on good edges and toss a big move up to jug at lip.

❏ **29.** Traverse?

❏ **30.** ?

Hillcrest Boulders

The Hillcrest Boulders host the test-piece of the area: Scott's Traverse. The original low and direct method goes at V9 or V7 with all holds. Enter the Open Space through the cow proof entry in the fence next to the boulder and head up the hill just a short three to five-minute walk to the left (south) to the good warm ups on the Mad Cow Boulder. About a five-minute walk uphill from the Mad Cow Boulder toward the saddle in the mountain is the Saddle Boulder with the classic Y-Crack. From the Saddle Boulder hike up the steep hill to the right (southwest) to the Forty Oz. Boulder and just a bit farther uphill after a total of about 15 to 20 minutes of uphill hiking from the car is The Mother, standing proud on top of the highest hill with 360 views. GPS Parking on Hillcrest Drive: 38.3938, -121.985183

Scott's Boulder

❏ **31. Scott's Traverse V7 or V9★★★** Start on the far left side and traverse right, staying below the double side-pulls on #33 for the original V9 version or use them and all the holds for the V7. Continue to traverse right past the steep shady face with problems #32–#34 and stay low to turn the corner into #35 and do it with a pump to finish. FA: Scott Frye.

❏ **32. V4★★** Sit start on good edges in a scoop and go up left.

❏ **33. V4★★** Sit start same as #32 but go right and up the face following zig zag seam.

❏ **34. V2★★** Stand start, then pull onto the mossy slab/face.

❏ **35. V4★★** Start at the right corner of the main boulder face and diagonal traverse up and right onto the slabby backside to finish.

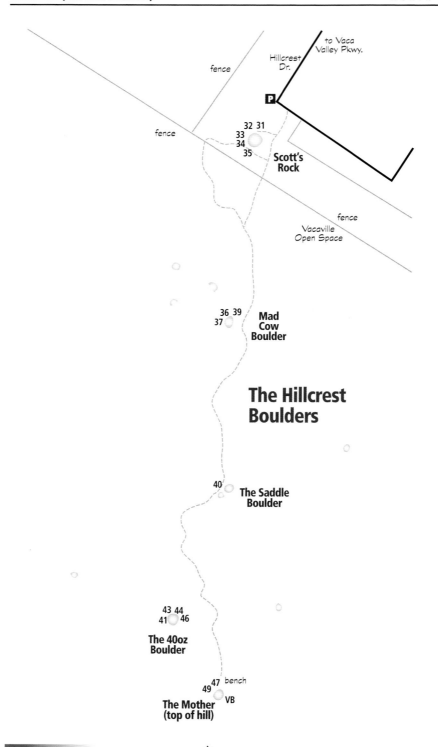

to Vaca
Valley Pkwy.

Hillcrest
Dr.

fence

P

fence

32 31
33
34
35

**Scott's
Rock**

fence

Vacaville
Open Space

36 39
37

**Mad
Cow
Boulder**

The Hillcrest
Boulders

40

**The Saddle
Boulder**

43 44
41   46

**The 40oz
Boulder**

47 bench
49

**The Mother
(top of hill)** VB

Mad Cow Boulder

❑ **36. Naked Lunch** V3★★ Sit start center of face.

❑ **37. Howling Mad** V0★★ Stand. V1 Sit. Arête in center of traverse.

❑ **38. Mad Cow Traverse** V2★★ Stand start usually done from left to right (although good in both directions) across horizontal rails and edges around arête (#37).

❑ **39.** V0-★★ Stand start left face.

The Saddle Boulder

❑ **40. Y-Crack** V0/V0+★★ V0 Left or V0+ Right. The splitter Y-shaped crack on the north side of the boulder is easily visible as you walk up the hill from Mad Cow Boulder in the saddle of the hillside along the trail up to the Forty Oz. Boulder and The Mother. **V2 Variation:** Sit start Y-cracks. **V3 Variation:** Sit start the steep face right of Y-Crack.

Forty Oz. Boulder

❑ **41. , Forty Oz. Traverse** V6★★★ Stand start on the far right side of the northwest face (right of #43), then traverse left past #43–#46 to the pumpy finish, pulling over the far left side.

❑ **42.** V0+★ Stand start same as #43, then bail up and right after the initial moves.

❑ **43. Gimme My Forty Sucka** V1★★★ Stand start on good diagonal edges just below a diagonal seam on the vertical face. Follow the seam up left to highball topout. Sit start is V3.

❑ **44. Brass Monkey** V2★★ Arête/face. Still a little dirty but with some more traffic it and #45 will soon be classic. V4 Sit start matched on in-cut right hand edge.

❑ **45. Natural Disaster** V2★ Stand start on the face ten feet left of arête (#44) on a flat left hand jug and go up the slightly overhanging loose and dirty (but fun) face. V4 Sit start #44 then traverse up and left into the stand start of #45.

❑ **46. V2 or V3**★★ V2 way: Sit start matched on good left hand edge just right of diagonal seam and follow the seam straight up past a big flat hollow hold to topout. V3 way: Same sit start, then diagonal up left before the big hold past crimpers.

The Mother

GPS: 38.387783, -121.992717

❑ **47. Mother Nature** V1R★★★★ Stand start just left of the north arête/prow and climb up the left side of the prow to an exciting highball topout. V3 Sit start on low left hand lay-back. Your Mother V2 Same sit start, then traverse up left over rocks into the 5.5 down climb.

❑ **48. Motherfucker Traverse** V4-V5★★★ V4 High – V5 Low Same sit start as #50, then traverse left and up around the prow (#47) on horizontal rails, then down a move into Your Mother to finish. **V5 Low Variation:** Same start, then stay below the horizontal jug rails on #47 into the same finish.

❑ **49. Space Lord** V1★★★ Stand start center of highball northwest face. V2 Sit start on a good flat left hand edge and right hand on a brown scarred edge.

❑ **50. Crispy Critters** V2★★ Sit start on the right side of the main face and go up flaky, lichen-covered crimper edge face.

Berkeley

Problems: **80**	
Rock: **Rhyolite**	
Difficulty: **VB-V13**	

Berkeley has seen it all. From old school soldiers in the war of gravity to modern day dreadlocked rock stars, they have all found many worthy challenges on the volcanic crags and boulders in the eucalyptus forests of the Berkeley hills. From the free belay evolution in the 1920s at Indian Rock to the free speech movement of the 1960s at UC Berkeley, all the way to the modern day free climbing movement of the 1990s at Mortar Rock, Berkeley has always been on the cutting edge. Some of the pioneers of rock climbing in Yosemite got their start and much needed practice on these small cliffs and boulders.

Indian Rock Park is the most popular crag, with perpetual visitors on top enjoying one of the best views of the Bay and almost as many visitors down below in The Pit enjoying the fine bouldering. Most of the crags and boulders are in parks with benches to relax on and groomed landings of wood chips or nice flat sidewalks. My grandfather Jack was born and raised in Berkeley in the 1920s. He used to tell me how he and a few friends would hike from their homes at sea level all the way up to Grizzly Peak. They would stop by Indian Rock to have lunch and check out the great view, which even then was a popular place to enjoy the scenery. He said Indian Rock had only one small farm house near it with a bunch of chickens that would run all over the old dirt roads.

Scott Frye on his classic Scott's Arête (V5).

About the rock

The 100 million-year-old volcanic rhyolite is colored whitish gray and has pockets, jugs, crimper edges, and cracks. Most of the climbs are so well traveled that anything loose has probably already broken off. However, still look out, especially if you get off the beaten track.

Because of the ratio of rock to climbers in the East Bay, The Pit at Indian Rock has become an outdoor gym. Most of the problems are vertical to slightly overhanging and have so many eliminate variations that a whole separate guidebook would be needed just to describe the better half of them. Get a local to show you the exact beta for the contrived eliminates. There are a few classic eliminates like Nat's Traverse, Bubble

Number of problems by difficulty

VB	V0	V1	V2	V3	V4	V5	V6	V7	V8	V9	V10	≥V11
7	13	8	3	12	6	5	5	7	6	3	0	5

Bypass, and White Men Can Jump. In fact, before City Rock (Berkeley's first climbing gym) opened around 1990 it seemed like the afternoon bouldering crowd in The Pit was a bit bigger and the eliminates a bit more appealing.

The most difficult boulder problems in the Bay Area, including Chris Sharma's newest test-piece known as The Impossible Traverse (V13), are all on Mortar Rock.

When to climb

All year is usually all good. The rock dries fast after winter rain storms and when the coast is wet and Castle Rock is still drying Berkeley can be the best alternative. Summer days can be hot unless there are cool Bay breezes and fog. Spring and fall are mostly all good with temps in the 60s to 70s.

Driving Directions

From the North Bay (US-101 in San Rafael) take I-580 over the Richmond/San Rafael Bridge and go a few miles southeast to just before the merge with I-80 and take the Albany/Buchanan St. exit.

From the East (Vallejo/Sacramento area) take I-80 west to the Albany/Buchanan St. exit which is near the I-580 merge just north of Berkeley.

From the South Bay (San Jose area) take I-880 north to I-580 north in Oakland. Continue north on I-580 (I-80 east) past Oakland to Berkeley and take the Albany/Buchanan St. exit. Make sure not to cross over the Bay Bridge on I-80 west (doh).

From San Francisco take I-80 over the Bay Bridge and go a few miles north on I-80 to the Albany/Buchanan St. exit.

Joel Booth on Nat's Traverse (V8). Photo by Chris McNamara.

From the Albany/Buchanan St. exit head east on Buchanan St. past San Pablo Ave. Buchanan St. turns into Marin Ave., follow Marin Ave. east into the hills. Drive uphill on Marin Ave. past The Alameda and the next major intersection will be the unique Europeon style driving circle. After negotiating (surviving) The Circle (hint: counterclockwise) either drive up one of the steepest roads in the Bay Area, Marin Ave. to Remilard Park

and Grizzly Peak Boulders or go just a short ways up Indian Rock Ave. to Indian Rock Park, which will be on your left. Arlington is just below Indian Rock Ave. and will take you to the Little Yosemite Boulders. From The Circle follow separate directions for each area.

GPS The Circle: 37.89, -122.271917

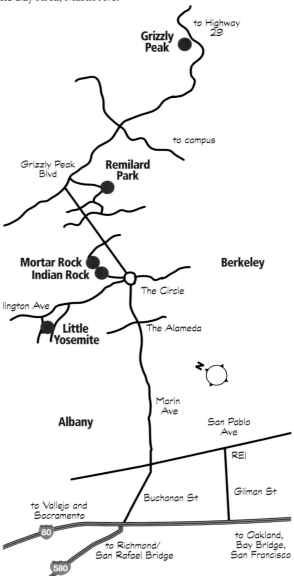

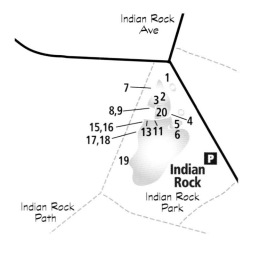

❏ **4. V2★★** Stand start arête in gully. **Off The Couch V4:** sit start on flat rock left of arête. **Couch Surfing V5:** same start as the V2 arête, then traverse low and left past the start of Off The Couch into a V0 finish on the far left side over rocky gully.

❏ **5. V0★★** Sit start small boulder.

❏ **6. V0★★** Slab face south of #5.

❏ **7. The Slab 5.4R★★** Stand start at the base of the stairs and go up the center of the slab face. No Hands Slab is 5.6r.

❏ **8. Center Overhang V3★★★** Stand start on a huge foot ledge on the left side wall of The Pit and go up the center of the highball overhang to the jug at the lip. **C+ Dyno V6:** Lunge from jug to jug.

❏ **9. 5.7★★** Stand start right of #8 up jugs.

❏ **10. Embryonic Journey V1★★★** Stand start just left of the chimney/corner, then pull onto the slab and highball up left or top out direct through the birth canal. **Edge Direct V2:** Sit start on sloper.

Indian Rock

Berkeley's most popular crag. From The Circle take Indian Rock Ave. uphill about one block to Indian Rock Park, which will be on your left. Walk down the stairs on the north side of the park to The Pit where most of the problems are found. Don't miss the awesome view from the top of the crag, just follow the steps carved into the stone on the south east side. GPS: 37.8924-122.272867

❏ **1. The Ape V1★★** Sit start on horizontal rails and go up short overhang above the sidewalk. **The Ape Traverse V3** Same sit start but traverse low crack left into the 5.4 slab topout over the sidewalk.

❏ **2. The Block V4★★** Traverse left to right on small boulder above rocky slab. **V0 Stand** start on horns and go up arête/prow.

❏ **3. The Seam V7★★** Sit start matched on a low right hand gaston/left hand lie-back crack. Make a few hard moves up past the seam crux, then onto the extremely highball (but easier) slab.

Sarah Gale on The Block (V0).

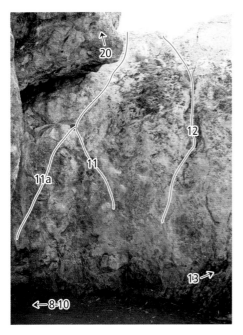

17. The Flake V3★★★ Stand start on the right side of the steep face and diagonal traverse up and left along good in-cut flake.

18. The Bubble V5★★★ Stand start at the base of The Flake and do tenuous moves up past the bubble-like pocket and over the highball finish. FA: Nat Smale, 1970s. **Bubble Bypass V6 Variation:** Skip the bubble-like pocket and lunge from the start to the mini jug.

19. Indian Rock Traverse V5★★ Start on the far bottom right (northwest) side of Indian Rock and traverse left and up past #18-#8 into #7. **V6 Variation:** Finish on #8.

20. I-12 V2/3X★★ Steep highball boulder solo or 5.11 toprope. Bolts are usually on top but you may need to bring hangers.

11. Watercourse V1★★★★ Stand start on the right side of the chimney and go up into the highball watercourse finish. **11a:** V3 Direct sit start or V0 Far left.

12. Beginners Crack V0★★★ Start right of #11 on good edges and go up face/crack.

13. Transportation Crack 5.4★★★★ Start right of #12 and left of arête. Go up the low-angle, well-featured slab crack to a high topout with a view. Down climb or walk off.

14. Indian Arête V0★★★ Stand start on Pegboard (#15) and climb up and left around arête onto slab topout.

15. Pegboard V1★★★ Stand start on huge jug rail and go up the slightly overhanging edges.

16. White Men Can Jump V7★★ Dyno all the way from the jug rail start of Pegboard past the good holds to the last in-cut mini jug near the top of the overhang.

Angie Corwin on Pegboard (V1).

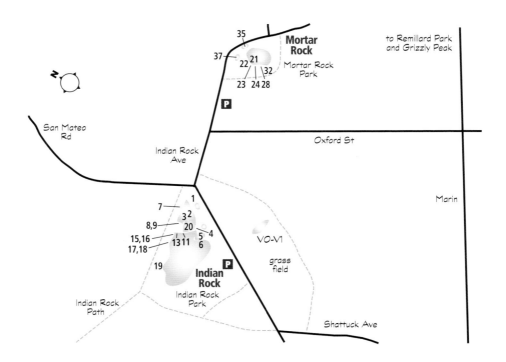

Mortar Rock

The Bay Area's most difficult boulder problems are found on the west face of Mortar Rock. From The Circle take Indian Rock Ave. uphill past Indian Rock Park on your left and continue uphill to just past Oxford St. where you can see Mortar Rock above the road to the right. Park on the street between the two parks and access them both. GPS: 37.893433 -122.272533

❏ **21. Nat's Traverse V8**★★★★ Stand start on the slabby left side of Mortar Rock and traverse right, staying low around the first corner below the jug rail past the first gaston crux to an OK under-cling rest in the corner. Continue traversing right around the powerful bulge, using either the rose move or the heelhook beta into The Ramp (#24) to finish. FA: Nat Smale, 1976.

Natural Nat's V7 Variation: Nat's Traverse with all holds, namely the jug rail at the start. Nat's Traverse backwards from The Ramp start is V7. From New Wave start is V9. **Marks Traverse V11**: Start from the jug on Don't Worry Be Snappy and go into Nat's Traverse in reverse.

❏ **22. V0**★★ Stand start in the corner of Nat's Traverse just right of the tree and go up the crack. V1 Low start from the under-cling hold on Nat's.

❏ **23. The Brink V4**★★ Sit start, crank past gaston crimp up into the jugs on the bulge in the center of Nat's Traverse and pull onto the (usually dirty) slab.

Chris Sharma on his Bay Area testpice The Impossible Traverse (V13fa). Photo by Jim Thornburg

❏ **24. The Ramp** V4★★★★ Stand start on good slot pockets and do a move up to the ball, then past the cheese-grater to the jug at the topout. Sit start V5. If you see chalk all over a bunch of little holds just right of The Ramp, you're looking at the old school eliminate Jungle Fever V8. All the good holds on The Ramp are off.

❏ **25. New Wave** V9★★★ Stand start on crimpy left hand under-cling and right hand sloper and go up. **The Kraken** V11: sit start. FA: Greg Loh.

❏ **26. Don't Worry Be Snappy** V12★★★ Stand start on obvious in-cut jug and try to go up. FA: Tom Richardson. **V12/13 Variation:** sit start on The Kraken. FA: Randy Puro.

❏ **27. The Impossible Traverse** V13★★★★ Same stand start as #26 on in-cut jug, then angle up and right into The Impossible Wall (#28) to finish. The hardest boulder problem in the Bay Area... so far. FA: Chris Sharma, 2004.

❏ **28. The Impossible Wall** V8★★★★ High stand start (pad stack) on left hand pinch/edge and right hand crimp edge and stick a few moves up past small in-cut pockets into the highball topout. Mission Impossible V9

Low stand start on right hand under-cling and left hand side-pull and pull down a couple hard moves into Impossible Wall. FA: John Sherman, 1980.

❏ **29. Chinese Connection** V12★★ low sit start to Mission Impossible (#28). FA: Greg Loh.

❏ **30. Beached Whale** V7★★ Stand start on a hollow flake a few feet right of #28 and go up right onto slab face left of #31. The sit start is V9.

❏ **31. Nat's Crack** V0R★★ Stand or sit start the crack in front of the bench.

❏ **32. Bench Wall** V2R★★★ Sit or stand start just right of the crack (#31) and go up the slightly overhanging face to a highball finale.

❏ **33.** V3★★ Stand start. Corner/arête to highball face. Right of #32.

❏ **34.** V0★ Face over stairs.

❏ **35. Little Half Dome** V1★★ Stand start in center of face over sidewalk.

❏ **36. Little Half Dome Traverse** V0★★ Start on either side and traverse the face.

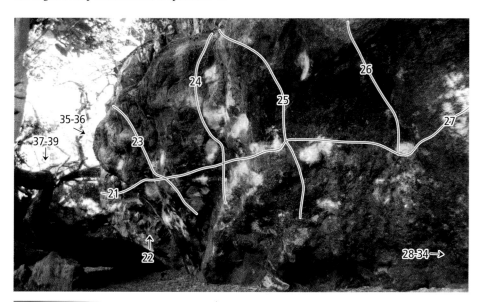

❏ **37. The Sidewalk Traverse V1**★★ Stand start on the right side and traverse the sloper lip up and left over the sidewalk. Always be respectful of passersby.

❏ **38. Pipeline Traverse V6**★★ Sit start low on the right side of #37 and traverse low across the face, staying below the lip.

❏ **39. The Girls Problem V5**★★ Stand start in the center of #37 + #38 (the face over the sidewalk) and go up slopey crimps.

Little Yosemite (aka Stoneface Park)

Take Arlington Ave. north from The Circle to a strange left turn for Yosemite Rd. (be careful crossing oncoming traffic and go a short way to a right turn onto Contra Costa Ave.). Little Yosemite is in a small dog park with a grassy field on the corner of San Fernando. Park on either San Fernando or around the corner on Thousand Oaks. GPS: 37.896783, -122.2782 Problems are listed counterclockwise.

❏ **40. The Great Stone Face V7**★★★★ Sit start on the steep prow on a right hand lie-back rail and crank up and left over bulge to topout. V4 Stand start on left hand edge. FA: Jim Thornburg, V4 Stand start late 80s. V7 Sit start, Phil Heller, early 90s.

❏ **41. Hoop Dreams V4**★★ Sit start on crimper under-clings just right of #40 and slam dunk the first move.

❏ **42. 5.7**★★ Short face right of #41.

❏ **43. V0**★★ High and steep slab face.

❏ **44. V3**★★ Sit start on small but good edges and bust a couple moves up and over bulge into slabby corner.

❏ **45. V?** Go up bulge past tiny edges.

❏ **46. V1**★ Sit start into bushy crack.

❏ **47. V1**★★ Sit start on good edges, then up over bulge into corner.

❏ **48. V3**★★ Stand start left of #40 on small edges. The sit start is a project.

❏ **49. V0**★ Stand start on small overhanging boulder next to the little building.

Remilard Park

From The Circle Head up the steep Marin Ave. crossing over Spruce St., then take a right on Regal. Cross over Euclid and continue uphill on Regal to Hilldale Ave. Turn left on Hilldale Ave. and go one block to Poppy Ln., then turn right and drive less than a 1/4 mile to the park on the right. GPS: 37.892417, -122.261083

❏ **51. Plaque Face V3R**★★ Stand start just right of the plaque and ascend the center of the face. Plaque Traverse V1 Traverse the plaque face in either direction.

❏ **52. Finger Crack 5.9X**★★ Start on face and make moves up into the diagonal finger crack/corner over the bad rocky landing. Should probably be toproped.

❏ **53. The Roof V0R/X**★★ Highball/5.10 toprope.

❏ **54. Direct Prow V0R**★★ Stand start right of the Bucket Prow (#55) and make a few moves up into the 5.6R/X (#55) to finish.

❏ **55. Bucket Prow 5.6R/X**★★★★ Stand start in big buckets and follow the line of buckets all the way up the steep highball prow. Old school belay pole on top.

❏ **56. V1R**★★ Face start, then up and right into prow (#55) to finish. **V2R/X Variation:** Same start but stay in the center of the face and finish direct.

❏ **57. Remilard Traverse V1**★★ Traverse between the left side of Remilard Rock and #55. **The Foolish Traverse V3:** Start same as #57, then traverse past the Bucket Prow (#55) under The Roof and up around the final corner to the overhanging finish.

❏ **58. Triangle Face** V3★★ Stand start.

❏ **59.** V1★★ Traverse usually done from right to left. V3 Dyno to the huge hueco.

Cragmont Park

Cragmont is just past Hilldale on Regal near Remilard Park. They are connected with the Pinnacle Path.

❏ **60. Gomer's Pile** V6★★ Traverse small overhanging boulder from right to left. GPS: 37.892717, -122.255367

Grizzly Peak

From The Circle, go up Marin Ave. to the top and turn right onto Grizzly Peak Blvd. About two miles south of Marin just past Centennial you'll see the boulders on the left (northeast) side of Grizzly Peak Blvd. There is NO PARKING on the sides of Grizzly Peak Blvd. from April 15 to November 15 due to fire hazard. Parking is allowed about ¼ mile down the road in either direction. My favorite is to the southeast in a large dirt pullout. GPS: 37.8755, -122.24155

❏ **61.** 5.6★★ Stand start on narrow juggy face between arêtes. V0 Sit start.

❏ **62.** V6★★ Low right hand sit start to #61. Scrunchy, powerful one-move wonder.

❏ **63. Scary Arête** V3★★★ Stand start on a good left hand gaston pocket (same as #64), then go up past the awesome sinker pockets that are shared by #64. Past the pockets take a hard left and reach out to the left arête, pull around and finish on #61.

❏ **64. Scary Overhang** V5★★★★ Stand start on a good left hand gaston pocket same as #63, then pull past sinker pockets straight up over the bulgy highball topout. Not as scary as it used to be since the huge rock under the landing was moved back and with the modern day use of crash pads. V8 Sit start on tiny gaston crimps and bust a couple hard moves up into the stand start.

❏ **65. Scott's Traverse** V7★★★ Stand start same as Scott's Arête (#66) on the cow udder but traverse left into #63 or #64 to finish. V8 sit start on far right.

❏ **66. Scott's Arête** V5★★★★ Stand start with right hand on the cow udder-shaped hold and left hand on a little hold low on the other side of the arête. Reach out left to the under-cling side-pull, then do big moves up the left side of the arête. Utterly wonderful. V6 Sit start with left hand in good low pocket. FA: Scott Frye, late 80s.

❏ **67. Direct Arête** V7★★★ Same stand start on the cow udder then go straight up past tiny edges to a lone jug on the lip of the overhang. V8 Sit start same as Scott's Arête.

❏ **68. Wandering Arête** V6★★★ Stand start (same as #69) on the sloper edges right of the cow udder hold on #66 and make a move past the under-cling pocket and past the small diagonal edges, then up and left to the lone jug on #67 and topout. V7 sit start.

❏ **69. Scott's Roof V6★★** Stand start on the sloper edges right of the cow udder-shaped hold on #66 and make a move past an under-cling pocket and up past the small diagonal edges to topout direct and right. V7 Sit start on good low pocket same as #66.

❏ **70. 5.7★★** Stand start. Climb the right or left side of slabby face.

❏ **71. Grizzly Peak Traverse V7★★** Stand start on horizontal edges on vertical face on the far left (same as #72), then traverse right around the arête/corners, staying below the lip all the way to the topout up and right of #75. Backwards V6 from sit start of #75. V4 Same start as #71 and #72, then traverse right around the arête/corners using all holds on the sloper lip and finish on the far right. Or do a 360.

❏ **72. V0★★** Stand start with good horizontal edges on vertical face and go up.

❏ **73. V4★★** Sit start on arête down and right of the stand starts for #71 and #72 and go up and left. V3 Right sit start on good in-cut pocket/under-cling and go up over knobby topout in center of face.

❏ **74. V1★★** Low stand start on good pockets just left of the right arête and just right of #73. Pull up onto slab to finish.

❏ **75. V3★★** Sit start on horizontal edges on far right side of boulder and go up past key hole slot.

❏ **76. V3★★** Stand start with a good four finger pocket and go up and right. V4 if you traverse from left start on flake. V0R if you stand start flake and go up over bad landing.

❏ **77. V3★★** Sit start on good right hand pocket and reach or dead-point up and left to the arête, then top out slab. **V2 Arête Variation:** Sit start on arête, left of the pocket sit start for the V3 and go up and right along the arête into stand start. V0 Stand start on arête and top out high slab.

❏ **78. Ejection Seat V1★★** Sit start on good holds low on the lip of the left arête/corner and go up. Slip and you eject into the gully.

❏ **79. Mike's Face V4★★** Stand start on small but good edges and go up the center of the face. V5 sit start same as #80 on low pocket.

❏ **80. Stink Bomb V3★★** Stand start, ascend right arête. The sit start is V4.

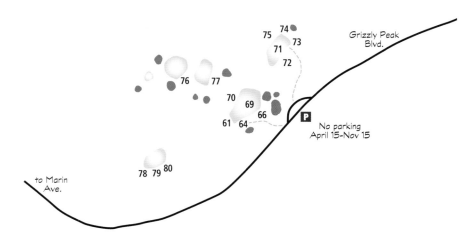

Glen Canyon Park

Problems: **20**

Rock: **Chert**

Difficulty: **VB-V4**

In the heart of the big city of San Francisco, a relatively quiet, forested canyon with a few chert cliff bands can be found only a mellow ten-minute stroll from the car down a nice, flat, shady trail. It is the only (and therefore the best) bouldering in the city and even has good parking. Climbers have been scaling rocks in the park since at least the 1930s and probably even longer than that. Rock climbing at Glen Canyon Park was even mentioned in the Sierra Club newsletter, The Yodeler, in 1940. No big V-grades to be bagged here, but a long, pumpy traverse and a lot of fun, moderate highballs should quench your thirst for stone. The unique Radiolarian Chert is neat to look at, let alone grab onto and climb. Perfect cracks and finger slots cover most faces and allow many options for hand and foot holds.

Mike Whipple enjoys Jugs (V1).

About the rock

The red chert can be solid in places but also hollow and loose in others, so be careful. Its many unique folds and layers offer good grips and provide a glimpse as to how the rock was formed on the ocean floor millions of years ago. The holds on most of the problems are a mix of edges, big flat chunks and the classic chert hold—the horizontal fingertip slot. Most of the problems overhang slightly but there are at least a few problems of every angle to play on. If you see tiny holds chalked up next to big holds it's because a few extremely strong locals have made up hundreds if not thousands of harder eliminates over the years. Unnatural Act is a popular highball problem (or toprope) that goes direct out the steepest section of a big roof on the rock on the hill behind the main cliff.

When to climb

All year round good conditions can be found. San Francisco gets rain throughout the winter (October to April) but the rock dries in a few hours of sunlight and can be climbable in less than a day after a rain. Summer can sometimes be hot (80s to 90s) but the fog usually hangs around and chills everything out. Spring and fall are the most consistent, with a nice mix of sun, fog, and only a little bit of rain.

Number of problems by difficulty

VB	V0	V1	V2	V3	V4	V5	V6	V7	V8	V9	V10	≥V11
5	10	3	1	1	1	0	0	0	0	0	0	0

Driving Directions

GPS Lower Canyon Parking at Elk St.:
37.736167, -122.439667

Glen Canyon Park is inside the San
Francisco city limits, southwest of the busy
downtown area.

Coming from downtown head west on
Market St. until it turns into Portola Dr.,
then near the Twin Peaks area take a left
onto O'Shaughnessy. Follow O'Shaughnessy
downhill to parking on either Bosworth
St. or Elk St.. Enter the park and head
northwest along a flat dirt path, passing a
school on your left and the Kung Fu Bridge
(got its nickname because a scene from the
TV show "Kung Fu" is rumored to have
been filmed here) just before the crags.

From the North Bay take US-101 over the
Golden Gate Bridge, then take a right after
the toll plaza onto CA-1/19th Ave.. Follow
19th Ave/Park Presidio Blvd. south through
Golden Gate Park and turn left onto Sloat.
Follow Sloat a short ways until it turns
into Portola, head uphill on Portola toward
Twin Peaks. At Twin Peaks turn right onto
O'Shaughnessy. Follow O'Shaughnessy
downhill to parking on either Bosworth
St. or Elk St.. Enter the park and head
northwest along a flat dirt path, passing a
school on your left and the Kung Fu Bridge
just before the crags.

From the East Bay, take I-80 over the Bay
Bridge into the city and through the Mission
District to I-280. Head south on I-280
toward Daly City for about 1.5 miles, then
exit onto Monterey Blvd. Take a sharp right
onto Monterey Blvd, then a left on Diamond
St. Turn left on Bosworth St. and park at the
intersection of Bosworth St. and Elk St. or at
the end of Bosworth St. near the Glen Park
Recreation Center. Enter the park and walk
northwest along a flat dirt path, passing a
school on your left and the Kung Fu Bridge
just before the crags.

From the South Bay take I-280 north into
San Francisco. Just past Daly City merge
onto San Jose Ave. and then take a right on
Rousseau St. and then a right on Bosworth
St. Park at the intersection of Bosworth
and Elk and enter the park or at the end of
Bosworth St. near the Glen Park Recreation
Center. Walk northwest along a flat dirt
path, passing a school on your left and the
Kung Fu Bridge just before the crags.

Upper Canyon Parking: Take Diamond
Heights Blvd. either downhill from Portola
(use Clipper St.) or uphill from Bosworth
and Elk to Berkeley Way and either park or
continue onto Crags Court and find parking
in the cul de sac and the trailhead to the
crags.

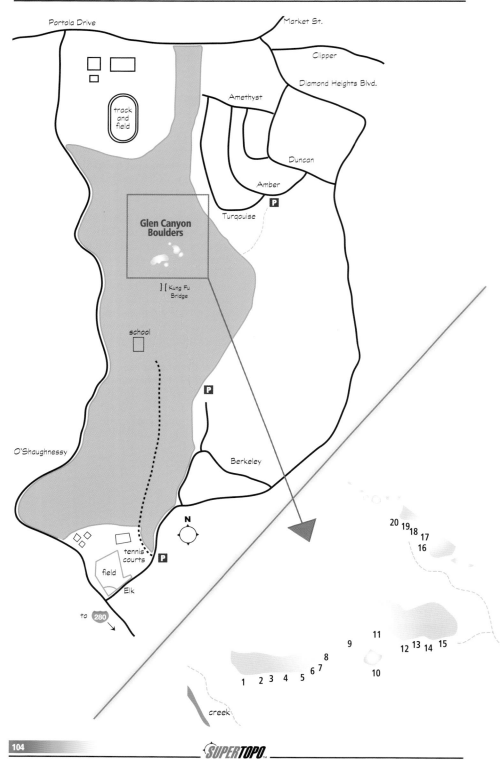

Main Face

GPS: 37.7421, -122.443683

❏ **1. Glen Park Traverse** V3★★★ Start on the left and traverse up and right across jug rails on a steep face around arête (#5) to walk off finish. Long and pumpy.

❏ **2.** V0+★★ Stand start then up the face/prow and top out right on #3.

❏ **3.** V0★★ Face to corner.

❏ **4.** V0-★★ Jugs.

❏ **5.** V1★★ Overhanging arête.

❏ **6.** V1R/X★ Start in the corner to the right of the finish of the traverse (#1) and go up the corner and along a left hand lieback crack to sketchy topout. Can also toprope.

❏ **7.** V0-R★★ Low left start to #8.

❏ **8. Lulu** 5.8R★★ Crack/face to highball bulge.

❏ **9.** 5.6★★ Dihedral.

❏ **10.** V3★★ V3 sit start arête. V4 sit start on left, then low traverse to the right into the sit start of the arête.

❏ **11.** 5,4R★★ Easiest way. Isn't that easy.

❏ **12. The Prow** V2★★ Steep prow with small sloper edges to jug horn and high topout. V2 traverse across the prow (#12) in either direction.

❏ **13. Jugs** V1★★ Overhanging jugs.

❏ **14.** 5.8★★ Classic old school crack/face.

❏ **15.** V0-★ Start on the far right side and pull up and around overhang on jugs.

Upper Cliffband - Unnatral Act

❏ **16.** V0-★★ Splitter highball crack.

❏ **17.** V1R★★ Highball stemming corner.

❏ **18. Unnatural Act (AKA Gunks Revisited)** V2R★★ Direct out center of huge roof. Toprope or highball/solo.

❏ **19.** V0★★ Chimney/stemming corner. Top out left into finish of #20. **V0+R Variation:** traverse under roof to highball finish of #18.

❏ **20.** V0★★ Stand start left arête. V1 Sit start. V4 traverse low and left from stand start of #18 past a pocket into V0 finish.

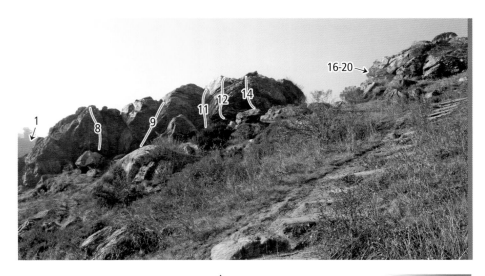

Castle Rock

Problems: 125

Rock: Sandstone

Difficulty: VB-V10, mostly V0-V9

John "Yabo" Yablonski works the project now called Groundation (V7)
Photo by Bruce Morris.

From back in the days of old school rock climbing pioneers such as Yabo and Cos to the new era of today's rock climbing stars such as Sharma, the enduring sandstone boulders of Castle Rock have been bouldering school for most local climbers. The Vaqueros Sandstone at Castle is like something out of another world. Honeycomb caves, sculpted arêtes, tafoni pockets, and strange cannonball shapes protruding from otherwise smooth blank walls of khaki stone all coalesce in your eyes, body, and mind, helping to relieve the boredom of the familiar, everyday world. The highest concentration of boulder problems in the Bay Area is side by side with great sport and trad crags. All this combined with legitimate access from one easily located parking area makes it the most popular all around rock climbing venue in the Bay Area. Unlike most of California's other, more vast bouldering areas, Castle doesn't have a mind blowing number of boulders, but what it may lack in quantity it more than makes up for in quality and tradition. Classics at every grade are usually no farther than a stone's throw from a trail, a crag, or the car. Just hiking around the rocks and scrambling in and out of the huge caves is enough fun for most visitors to the park, but if you crave even more of a challenge, then the plentiful selection of world class boulder problems should satisfy even the pickiest of stone crusaders.

About the Rock

The sandstone at Castle Rock is similar to the sandstone at the world renowned Fontainbleau, France. Odd friction moves and straightforward power moves are the norm. Trusting flat smears while hanging from tilted sloper handholds is a delicate and powerful game that involves many different skills. Mentally it requires imagination, commitment, and timing. Physically, skills such as strength, flexibility, and balance are all required to ascend these unique bouldering challenges. Technique will get you much higher than brute strength. Finesse and body English are the keys to success on these subtle classics.

Number of problems by difficulty

VB	V0	V1	V2	V3	V4	V5	V6	V7	V8	V9	V10	≥V11
3	12	15	10	20	20	9	8	5	5	5	3	0

When to climb

The big slopers and small edges feel better on cool, dry days when the skin is grippin' and the rubber is stickin'. Winter obviously has the best cold conditions, but they are few and far between during a lot of wet, rainy days. The soft sandstone absorbs and holds rainwater, and shade from the thick forest that surrounds the rock causes the stone to dry slowly, much more slowly than most other rocks. Give the boulders three to five days to dry after a rain before you climb on them, depending on how much it rained and how sunny and windy it got after the rain. Sandstone is brittle; damp sandstone is more brittle. You should not only be careful of holds breaking for your own safety, but much more importantly you should be careful not to break any of the precious holds on these classic boulder problems. If you do climb there too soon after a rain and break a hold on a classic, then you deserve to fall on your ass. Summertime can have the occasional heat wave with highs in the 90s. Be warned: mosquitoes and a lot of other bugs will be out enjoying the park during the summer months. Don't worry, spring and fall are full of perfect days with fewer crowds, fewer bugs, and sticky dry conditions with good temps in the 60s-70s.

Driving Directions

From the North Bay/San Francisco area take US-101 or I-280 to CA-85, then exit Saratoga Ave. and follow it southwest for about a mile to the fancy city of Saratoga. From Saratoga take CA-9/Big Basin Way west into the hills. After about ten miles you will be on top of the hills at the Saratoga Gap intersection with Skyline Blvd. (CA-35). Turn left (south) onto Skyline Blvd. (CA-35) and drive about two miles to the park on the right (west) side of the road.

From the South Bay/San Jose area take US101 or I280 to Highway 85, then exit Saratoga Ave. and follow it southwest for about a mile to the city of Saratoga. From Saratoga take Highway 9/Big Basin Way west into the hills. After about ten miles you will be on top of the hills at the Saratoga Gap intersection with Skyline Blvd. (CA35). Turn left (south) onto Skyline Blvd. (CA35) and drive about two miles to the park on the right (west) side of the road.

From the East Bay/Oakland area take I-680 or I-880 south to San Jose. From I-680 in San Jose take I-280 northwest to CA-17. From I-880 and CA-17 in San Jose follow CA-17 south about four miles to Highway 85. Take CA-85 northwest to Saratoga Ave. and follow it southwest for about a mile to the city of Saratoga. From Saratoga take CA-9/Big Basin Way west into the hills. After about ten miles you will be on top of the hills at the Saratoga Gap intersection with Skyline Blvd. (CA-35). Turn left (south) onto Skyline Blvd. (CA-35) and drive about two miles to the park on the right (west) side of the road.

From Santa Cruz take River St. northwest out of town. It will turn into CA-9. Follow Highway 9 to the top of the hills at the Saratoga Gap intersection with Skyline Blvd. (CA-35), turn right (south) onto Skyline Blvd. and drive about two miles to the park on the right (west) side of the road. Most of the boulder problems are scattered around the main Castle Rock formation, which is on the west side of Skyline Blvd. just a five to ten-minute hike uphill on the main trail from the parking lot.

Approach

Most of the boulder problems are scattered around the main Castle Rock formation, which is on the west side of Skyline Blvd. just a five to ten-minute hike uphill on the main trail from the pay parking lot. Parking on the side of Skyline Blvd. is free but there is no parking after dark or else you will be ticketed. Please obey all the rules and regulations of the park.

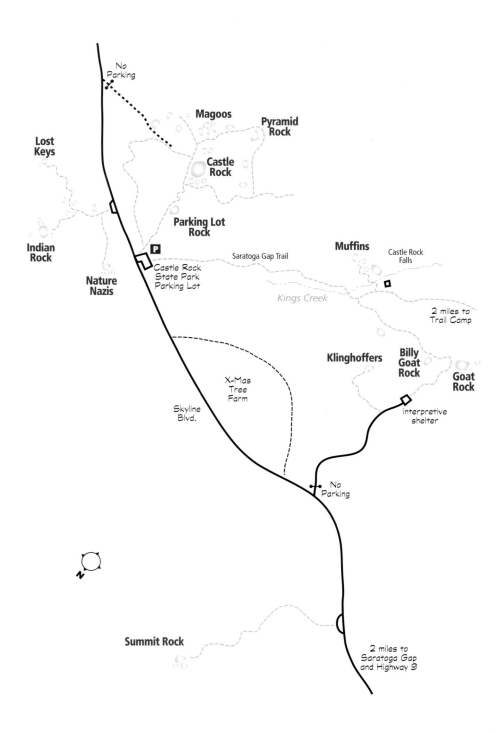

No Parking

Magoos

Pyramid Rock

Lost Keys

Castle Rock

Parking Lot Rock

Indian Rock

Saratoga Gap Trail

Muffins

Castle Rock Falls

Nature Nazis

Castle Rock State Park Parking Lot

Kings Creek

2 miles to Trail Camp

Klinghoffers

Billy Goat Rock

Goat Rock

X-Mas Tree Farm

interpretive shelter

Skyline Blvd.

No Parking

Summit Rock

2 miles to Saratoga Gap and Highway 9

Charlie Barrett on Pyramid Crack VOR.

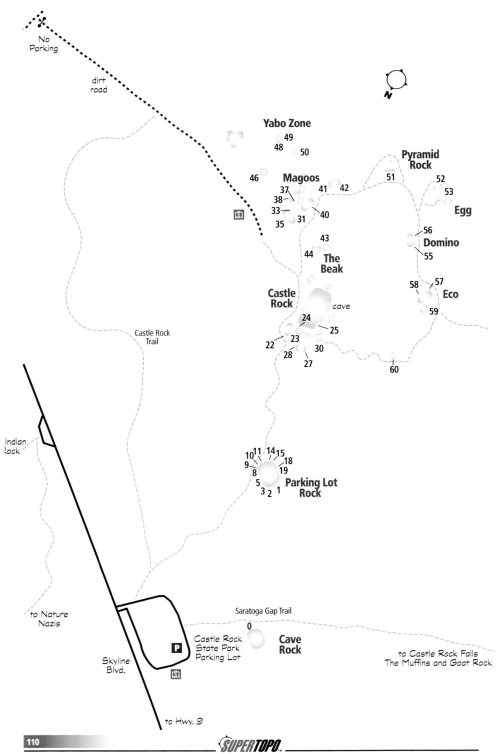

No Parking

dirt road

Yabo Zone

49
48   50

Pyramid Rock

46   Magoos
      37   41   42   51   52
      38   53
      33   31   40   Egg
      35

                                    56
                            Domino
                        55

43

44   The Beak

Castle Rock   cave
                                    58   57
                                        Eco
        24   59
22   23   25
28   30
    27   60

Castle Rock Trail

Indian Rock

        11 14 15
    10 / / / 18
9 / 8 /   19
        5
        3 2 1   Parking Lot Rock

to Nature Nazis

Saratoga Gap Trail
                    0
Castle Rock State Park Parking Lot   Cave Rock

P

Skyline Blvd.   to Castle Rock Falls
                                The Muffins and Goat Rock

to Hwy. 9

Parking Lot Boulder

One of the best boulders in Northern California. Problems from V0 to V10 surround this big blob of sculpted sandstone. The Yabo Cave on the southwest side of the boulder has a couple of the steepest and most classic problems in the park, Yabo Roof V5 and Coz Daddy V6 are some of the best of the original problems established by the famous old school Stonemasters. GPS: 37.229600, -122.095233

❏ **0. Groundation** V7★★★★
Classic highball face left of tree. This is on Cave Rock (next to the parking lot).

❏ **1.** V0-V3★★ Various slabby, mossy, semi highball problems can be done on the northwest face of Parking Lot Rock.

❏ **2. Parking Lot Traverse** V7★★ Traverse from the northeast corner (#3) uphill to the left past the starts of #4–#7 until it is possible to lean across to #8 and turn the corner past #9 and into #10 for the pumpy finale. V8 **Variation:** Start on slab face (#1).

❏ **3.** V4★★ Highball arête right of tree.

❏ **4.** V1★★ Pockety face with tree behind.

❏ **5. Flakes** V3★★★ Stand start on good right hand lay-back flake and ascend the highball face.

❏ **6. Let's Get Hurt** V3★★ Start in right facing jug and go up highball face left of #5. Back in the days before pads this may have got an R rating. Spotters can help keep you from sliding down the hill into the rocks.

❏ **7.** V1★★ Stand start on the far left side of the northeast face and go up pockets and slopers.

❏ **8. Girl Butter** V1★★ Stand start on the right side of the prow, just left of the corner.

❏ **9. Rug Head (AKA Rug Rat)** V2★★★★ Stand start in hueco under-clings on prow or from the same start as the Tree Route on the left. V3 sit start down and right on low under-cling jug same as the Tree Route.

❏ **10. Tree Route** V4★★★★ Stand start in hueco and go up left into highball groove. V5 Sit start down and right on low under-cling jug same as Rug Head.

❏ **11. Deforestation** V9★★★ Stand start on under-cling/gaston and crimp your way up. **Seven Arrows** V10: Straight up face between Collins Problem and Deforestation.

❏ **12. Collins Problem** V10★★ Stand start on thin (slowly getting thinner) crimper edges.

❏ **13.** V1★★ Stand start right hand on big lieback, then top out direct.

❏ **14.** V0★★★ Stand start on left hand lieback and right hand gaston.

❏ **15. Coz Mama** V4★★★ Sit start on good edge and slap slopers up over short bulge.

❑ **16. V4**★★ Sit start into slopers.

❑ **17. VB**★ Tiny, fun bear hug bulge.

❑ **18. Coz Daddy V6**★★★ Sit start on a big flat jug under the center of the roof and boulder up and right to the sloper arête, then pass the reachy pocket crux and topout. FA: Scott Cosgrove.

❑ **19. Yabo Roof V5**★★★★ Sit start in the cave and make your way up and out over the slopey lip. FA: John Yablonski.

❑ **20. V4**★ Mossy cracks left of tree and #19.

Castle Rock Boulders

These are some of the best problems in the park. New gems like Waimea Arête V6 just got unearthed right next to old classics like the highball Waimea Wall V1. The Spoon is another classic along with the sticky holds on Duct Tape Arête. Bates Arête never gets old and the Sharma Traverse is addictive once you learn the magic beta. GPS: 37.228650, -122.096200

❑ **21. The Frog Traverse V2**★★ Stand start the same as The Spoon, then traverse left across horizontal tips crack.

❑ **22. The Spoon V2**★★★ Stand start with the round under-cling pocket and pull straight out over the concave bulge onto the sloper topout.

❑ **23. V2**★★ Stand start around the corner to the right of The Spoon (#22) on thin edges on a steep, clean slab face and end in big hueco. Sit start is V5.

❑ **24. Duct Tape V5**★★★ Squat start with right hand low on the sloper arête and left hand low on a sloper side-pull fingertip under-cling.

❑ **25. Waimea Wall V1**★★★ Stand start right of the arête on the clean highball face. It is left of Farewell to Arms 5.9 toprope crack. Down climb left (5.6R).

❑ **26. Waimea Arête V6**★★★ Stand or sit start steep highball prow with slopey topout. The down climb for both Waimea problems is the 5.6R to the left.

❑ **27. Sharma Traverse V6 or V8**★★★ Start on the far right side (on #28) and traverse left, staying low across the short slab face around the corner to the final crux section. V6: Start on the jugs on or below the corner and just do the final crux section.

❑ **28. V3**★★ Ascend the steep, crimpy slab face on the northeast side of the boulder.

❑ **29. V0**★★ Small steep boulder with big sloper jugs left of Bates Arête.

❑ **30. Bates Arête V4**★★★ Sit start on sloper lip/arête and traverse up and left over rocky landing.

Magoos

Mr. Magoo was a crotchety, nearsighted, lovable old cartoon character from the 1950s. These fine boulders are by no means crotchety but they are old and lovable. This is definitely one of the best and therefore most popular places in the park to drop the pad and get busy. Centrally located, flat dirt landings, and more than enough classics from V0 to V10.

☐ 31. Bates Problem V6★★★
Stand start on small, slopey, crimper edges and bust a move up and left to the top: V6. Sit start is V9. **Bates Eliminate V7:** Stand start on the same holds but make a move up and right to a good edge, then left to the top: V7. **Bates Eliminate Sit V10:** Sit start on low sloper lieback. FA: Barry Bates.

☐ 32. V9/10★★ Stand start right of the tree on small sloper edges and do a couple moves up into the top of Mr. Magoo to finish. Rarely repeated.

☐ 33. Mr. Magoo V1★★★★ Stand start on slopey crimper edges and do a few moves up to and past a large brown plate-like jug into the easier yet highball finish.

☐ 34. V0★★ Stand start with a good slot pocket and go up groove past a knobby jug.

☐ 35. V0★★ Sit start under roof and ascend the right hand arête. The direct arête is V3.

☐ 36. V0★★ Sit start under roof, then move up and right out crack onto slab.

☐ 37. The Swim V3★★★ Stand start with under-cling horn and swim up over sloper topout.

☐ 38. Mrs. Magoo V2★★ Stand start to slopey, bulgy, slabby face left of corner.

☐ 39. The Roof V3★★ Start in cave right of The Swim and climb direct over the groovy roof in a tight corridor. **Kauk Roof V6/7 Variation:** Stay right of the juggy groove.

☐ 40. Dog Dish Traverse V2★★★ Stand start on the bottom right side and traverse up and left past the slippery "dog dishes" into the semi highball V0 Dog Dish finish.

☐ 41. The Slap V4★★★ Sit start on an under-cling knob, then pull out to and over the sloper right hand arête onto the "no hands slab." **The Slope V5:** Same sit start, then straight up.

☐ 42. Hueco Wall V5★★★★ Sit start with right hand in hueco and left on low edge – bump it up. Hueco Wall Traverse V8 Same sit start, then traverse below the lip to finish on the far left.

☐ 43. Asshole Arête V5★★ Sit start, then slap your way up the short sloper arête.

☐ 44. Beak Mantel V4★★ Stand start on the good holds below the beak and try to go up. Sit start is V5. Mantling direct on the beak is at least a grade harder.

☐ 45. Beak Traverse V3★★ Sit start on the left side of the Beak Boulder.

Yabo Zone

Only a short stumble downhill from the
Magoos, a few fun problems and a quiet
place to hang out.

❏ **46.** V1★★ Stand start highball north face.
V2 Sit start.

❏ **47.** V3★★ Traverse up and right around
corner into #46.

❏ **48. Sloper Arête** V3★★★ Stand start. The
low start is V5.

❏ **49. Tongue in Groove** V4★★ Stand start on
slopey lumps. The sit start is V5.

❏ **50.** V4★★ Sit start short overhanging
bulge.

The Graveyard

The piece de resistance of Castle Rock Park
is the Eco Terrorist, which looms over the
trail in the spooky Graveyard. The exciting
Pyramid Crack and the tricky Domino
Theory are also found here, right off the
trail, downhill, southwest of the main Castle
Rock formation.

❏ **51. Pyramid Crack** V0R★★★★ Diagonal
splitter highball crack. Down climb 5.6R.

❏ **52. Insecurian Arête** V4R★★ Ascend left to
right into high topout.

❏ **53. Egg Head Arête** V8★★ Sit start under
overhang, then climb up past big sloper.
V9 Sit start down and left, then traverse a
few moves up and right into the sloper crux.

❏ **54. Egg Head** V4★★ Traverse from the
good holds under the overhang to the left.

❏ **55. Domino Theory** V4★★ Traverse left to
right around corner over trail. Bad landing.

❏ **56. Domino** V2★★★ Center face over trail.
Bad landing. **V3 Variation**: dyno to jug at
lip. Very bad landing.

❏ **57. Eco Terrorist** V10★★★★ Stand start
in hueco, fire to slopey lip, bump past
slopers, pop to the huge hueco and finish:
magnificent. First attempted by the old
school (pre pad) crew back in the day and
written off as a Yabo "project" until the
aspiring young local Chris Sharma set it free
back in March 1997. FA: Chris Sharma.

❏ **58. Wish You Were Here** V9★★ Stand start
in under-clings and pull past right hand
pocket to sloper crux hueco finale. - or
Wish You Would Go V2 Variation: Low start
on far right side of rock into hueco finish.
FA: Bruce Morris.

❏ **59.** V10/11★★ Sit start then pull sloper lip
bulge onto slab top out. (behind Eco)

❏ **60.** V3★★ Sloper arête to lip mantle.

Castle Rock Falls / Muffins

A few good problems and a few short sport climbs are spread around the labyrinths of rock called The Muffins above and south of Castle Rock Falls. Find the overgrown approach trail just off of the main trail just before (east of) the observation platform on top of the falls. GPS Muffins: 37.225883, -122.104383

❏ **61. Pocket Face** V3★★★ Stand start on small pockets on a short steep face on the right side of the wall.

❏ **62. Sticky Green Traverse** V6★★ Start on the V3 (#61), then traverse left across the slopey lip to topout on the far left before the trees.

❏ **63.** V2★★ Sit start in the center of the Sticky Green Traverse and pull over the lip.

❏ **64. Pocket Change** V4★★ Stand or sit start on a small separated boulder and traverse left past the pocket change moves into the mossy offwidth crack (#65) to finish.

❏ **65.** V0★ Mossy offwidth crack left of short toprope face. Finish of traverse (#64).

❏ **66. Gym Rat** V5★★ Sit start, then go left and up the sloper arête. The stand start is V4. **Right V0 Variation:** Stand start then up right to topout. **Right V1 Variation:** Sit start then topout up and right.

❏ **67. Day Sleeper** V1★★ Sit start on under-cling and climb the face just left of the arête.

❏ **68. Grotesque Old Woman** V4R★★ A bad landing makes this fun pocket problem gnarly.

❏ **69. Devil Baby** V4★★ Stand start on brown knobs right of thread and make moves up left past huge hueco to sloper topout on ledge.

❏ **70. Muffin Master** V4★★ Stand start on good holds, then crank on a left hand gaston up and right to a jug and top out.

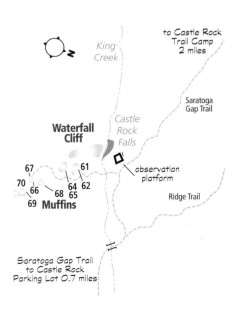

Rob Bianco on Pocket Change (V4).

Billy Goat Rock

A steep bouldering wall and a few sport routes in the 5.10 to 5.11 range hang over the trail just before Goat Rock. The classic V5 known as Way Dubious Contortionist and all its linkup variations are not to be missed. GPS Goat Rock: 37.2286, -122.107767

❏ **71. V0**★★ Stand start the right boulder.

❏ **72. V1**★★ Stand start the steep left boulder.

❏ **73. Projectile Vomit V3**★★★ Sit start with feet on big ledge and left hand in horizontal crack, then go up right side of overhanging face.

❏ **74. Way Dubious Contortionist V5**★★★ Stand start in overhead under-cling hueco pinch and contort your way up and out the overhang. Use a spotter when pulling on the hollow hold at the lip. V8 Low under-cling start into V5 hueco stand start. Technical Contortionist V6 Stand start same as Way Dubious Contortionist, then traverse right into Projectile Vomit to finish. V9 Do the low under-cling start into V6. FA: Dave Caunt.

❏ **75. Billy Goat Traverse V6**★★ Stand start on the left arête of the overhang, which is on the far right side of the face with the bolted sport routes. Traverse left across the face past the sport routes and step off on the far left side. Pumpy/technical.

Goat Rock

Only my favorite five problems are listed at Goat Rock because it is the furthest area from the car. There are actually enough problems on Goat and Billy Goat and on all the boulders in the forest around them to keep just about anyone busy for a day. Bring a rope and some gear to do the classic 75-foot tall 5.10 called the Great Roof on Goat Rock's main face.

❏ **76. Goat Rock Traverse V4**★★★ Traverse the southwest face. 100 feet. Often dry in a light rain.

❏ **77. Planet Caravan V6/7 or V8/9**★★★ **V6/7 way:** sit start on a good right hand edge and small left at the base of the steep wall and go up left, pulling on slopey scoops, close to the rock on the side. The rock to the left might be hit if you fall off the crux, so a spotter is helpful. **V8/9 Direct:** same sit start, then go direct, straight up center of thin face to sloper topout. FA: Jeremy Meigs.

❏ **78. V6**★★ Sit start same as Planet Caravan up to the good edges, then reach up and right to the crimpy horizontal seam, then traverse right into the top of #79.

❏ **79. V2**★★ Sit start on low left hand under-cling pocket and reach for jug and topout right. Direct topout onto sloper ledge is V3.

❏ **80. Bowling Ball V1**★★★ Stand start on pockety bulge over trail on top of Goat Rock. V2 Sit start or V0 Left stand start.

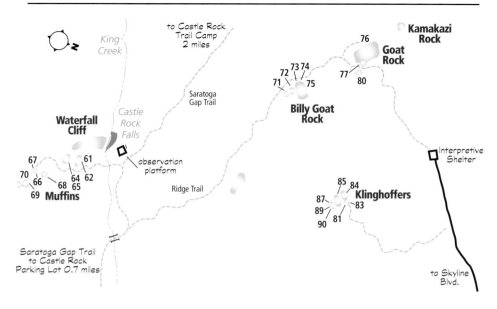

Klinghoffers

These heady test-pieces were put up in the late 70s/early 80s during a time referred to by locals as the Reign of Terror. They don't get repeated often, at least not without a toprope. The problems that aren't going to make you crap your pants are also really good. The pumpy and technical Klinghoffer Traverse V5 is one of the best in the park and the slopey and powerful Right Hand Man V7 is a new school classic. A bit hard to find but so worth it. GPS Klinghoffers: 37.228633, -122.104533

❏ **81. Right Hand Man V7★★★** Sit start crimping a left hand side-pull and right hand under-cling edge and do triple bumps up the sloper right arête and topout.

❏ **82. Left Hand Boy V1★★** Stand start on pockets left of Right Hand Man. V2 Sit start on left hand lieback jug.

❏ **83. Death Wish V4★★** Stand start right hand in pocket and pull mossy overhang. V5/6 Sit start on brown sloper right hand knob.

❏ **84. Coz Solo V3R/X★★★** Center of high face. Start on lie-backs and solo past huecos. Bolts on top. **Superman Was Out of Town V3R/X:** right of Coz Solo. These are proud lines that rarely get repeated, so they may be a bit dirty.

❏ **85. Klinghoffer Traverse V5★★★★** Start in two-finger left hand pocket and right hand side-pull and traverse uphill to the left along the base of the wall. **V6R Variation:** do the V5 into Man Overboard for a sporty finish.

❏ **86. Man Overboard V3R★★** Start in big hueco at end of traverse wall and go up.

❏ **87. Achilles Lauro V4★★★** Balancey arête.

❏ **88. Center Crack V1★★★** Right hand lieback flake left of arête.

❏ **89. Grey Face V1R★★** Climb up past big hueco to highball finish.

❏ **90. Oswald Cheese V3R★★** Climb the right side of face with pockets and huecos.

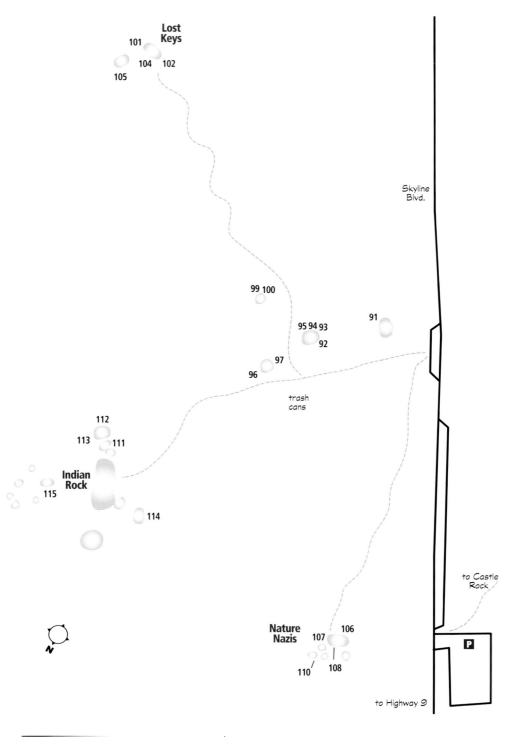

Lost Keys

101

104   102

105

Skyline Blvd.

99 100

95 94 93

92

91

97

96

trash cans

112

113   111

Indian Rock

115

114

N

Nature Nazis

107   106

110   108

to Castle Rock

P

to Highway 9

Indian Cracks

A couple of good cracks, some fun moderates, and a few short steep test-pieces are all a short walk from the parking lot. Not as crowded as the main Castle Rock area on busy weekends. GPS Indian Rock parking: 37.23005,-122.0938

❏ **91. Tafoni Baloney V1**★★ Roadside classic.

❏ **92. Indian Crack V0**★★★ Smooth and solid, good crack fun. Stand start crack or sit in hueco.

❏ **93. Honey Dipper V2**★★ Stand start with the left hand hueco and go up. V3 Sit start on funky dark brown under-cling. **Raw Honey V3 Variation:** stand start right hand on thin, crimpy tips lieback crack and left hand in side-pull hueco and go up direct. If you sit start under-cling it is V4.

❏ **94. 1 1/4" Crack V1**★★ Honest to goodness crack climbing, albeit a little short. Tough right hand lieback moves up the inch and a quarter crack.

❏ **95. Indian Traverse V5**★★ Start right of the 1 1/4" Crack in a big hueco and traverse left around the corner past Honey Dipper and end on Indian Crack.

❏ **96. Static Reach V8**★★ Sit start on a good edge at the base of a miniscule left hand arête, pull on and try to static the reach to the top. Much harder than it looks.

❏ **97. The Clam V3**★★ Sit start on a large bulbous left hand chunk under the right side of the mini cave and do a few moves up over the sloper lip onto the mossy slab to finish.

❏ **98. The Clam Traverse V9**★ Sit start same as The Clam and traverse left along the low sloper lip. Scrunchy and butt-dragger but good moves.

❏ **99. Red Knobs V2**★★ Stand start on good holds and pull/push your way past the Red Knobs.

❏ **100. V4**★★ Traverse from the sit start of Red Knobs to the left along slopey diagonal crack past huecos to topout in cleft.

Lost Keys Boulder

These five great problems are worth the short hike downhill from the Indian Cracks. Lost Keys Traverse is a perfect mix of pockets, slopers, and jugs. Definitely the best V6 traverse in the park.

❏ **101. Lost Keys Traverse V6**★★★★ Start on the left side of the Lost Keys boulder and traverse right into the Lost Keys problem to finish. FA: Jeremy Meigs.

❏ **102. Lost Keys V3**★★★ Sit start on good holds and go up and right to sloper topout.

❏ **103. Vicious V7**★★ Direct Variation to Lost Keys. Sit start right of Lost Keys, go straight out short overhang past pocket to sloper topout. Jugs on left are off.

❏ **104. V4**★★ Direct up highball face above the start of the Lost Keys Traverse.

❏ **105. V3**★★ Traverse smaller boulder opposite Lost Keys.

Nature Nazis

About five to ten easy to hard lowballs and a few highballs and traverses. Naturally sculpted edges and slopers on the awesome Caunt Power Pull and Nature Nazi Traverse are some of the finest in the park. There is a classic arête climb here but a big tree fell under it making it history, for now.

❑ **106. Caunt Power Pull** V4★★★ Stand start on powerful bear hug slopers, then hit the perfect sculpted edges on the lip and pull over onto the high mossy slab to finish. FA: Dave Caunt.

❑ **107. Nature Nazi Traverse** V4★★★ Stand start on the left side of the overhanging east face and traverse up right along smooth sloper lumps into the top of Caunt Power Pull to finish. **V2 Variation**: Start traverse, then top out.

❑ **108. Nature Nazi Arete** V7★★★★ Stand start to steep clean right hand arete.

❑ **109. Little Man in the Canoe** V3★ Low stand start with left fingers in crack and right hand smacking the cheek like sloper, top out up and left on slab.

❑ **110. V0**★★ Lieback with smears for feet. V5 Right start on slopers.

❑ **111. V0**★★★ Climb slabby arête on left boulder. The knobby slab on the right boulder is VB and equally as good.

❑ **112. F.F. Crack** V4★★ Sit start on right hand lieback, then traverse low and left across wide horizontal crack. V5 Right start with hand jam. V1 Sit start on the lieback then top out straight up.

❑ **113. Naked Nazi** V3★★★ Right hand arete past hueco to mantle top out - or Neo Nazi V6 start on face and make a thin/crimper move up right into Naked Nazi Arete to top.

Indian Rock

Old school classics, a couple of new test-pieces, fun sport climbs, and an escape

The classic Nature Nazi Arête near Indian Rock.

from the sometimes crowded main area are all just a short walk from the road. are two classics. At the base of Indian Rock is the short, fun Hash Rock with a few good problems all over fairly good landings. GPS Indian Rock: 37.231383, -122.093733

❑ **114. Wanker's Delight** V3★★ Sit start on slopey scoops and go up. V4 Direct.

❑ **115. The Classic** V3★★★★ Stand start in hueco, reach sloper lip and pull over. V4 Sit.

❑ **116. Sharma Arête** V9★★★ Stand start highball arête over potentially bad landing in a crevice filled with logs to support multiple pads. Spotters and pads a must.

❑ **117. Hash Rock** VB-V5★★ Short, fun boulder with a good landing and about five to ten excellent sit starts and one-move wonders. **The Under-cling V0** is a classic.

❑ **118. Santa Cruz Dude** V3★★★ Dyno. Stand start on good edges in the center of the clean face and lunge to the juggy lip.

Tree in the Wall

These cool newly discovered and developed boulders are about 2 miles south of the Castle Rock State Park Parking Lot - park in the Sanborn Skyline County Park parking lot on the left (east) side of Skyline and hike the main trail northeast about 5 minutes to the first boulders then the next boulders are a couple more minutes further down the trail to the right (VB-V8)

Upper Boulders

❏ **119. Tree in the Wall V4**★★★ Main highball face of tall boulder next to trail.

❏ **120. Skunkape Stem V5**★★★ Start in slabby stem and traverse up right past sloper hueco to top out arouund corner.

Lower Boulders

Main Boulder

❏ **121. V2**★★★ 3 variations: start at center/right and go direct over hueco bulge V2 or start on left and traverse sloper buckets up right to same top out V3 or traverse face low from left to right up into the main line V4!

❏ **122. V3**★★ Short sit start on small boulder right of main boulder?

Bastard Boulder

❏ **123. V0**★ Left side of short wall - a few variations - or sit start in pocket V4.

❏ **124. V5**★★★ Sit start in big hueco scoop and go direct up and over to top out!

❏ **125.Tall Bastard V8**★★★ Sit start in hueco and climb up reachy sloper left arete.

Andrew Zaslove on #121 at Tree in The Wall.

Aquarian Valley

Problems: **20**

Rock: **Sandstone**

Difficulty: **V0-V7**

A handful of intermediate to hard problems in a steep cave next to a waterfall. Sound good? It is. The cave is mostly shady in summer and it can sometimes stay dry in a light rainstorm in winter. Cool breezes blow up over the foothills from the not-so-distant ocean and the picturesque waterfall flows right next to the cave and offers a refreshing vibe of its own. The semi-long hike keeps the masses away, but for a psyched boulderer it is merely a warm up for the blood-pumping climbs inside the cave. Sinker pockets, nail biting edges and even a mini elephant trunk like tufa keep you clinging onto this overhung stone. Back when I found the cave around the turn of the century there was only a little bit of chalk on the starting holds of the Stoner Traverse but the rest of the problems seemed pretty much untouched. There was also only a little bit of stoner graffiti done mostly with black soot, so we gave it the nickname Stoner Cave (for that and 420 other reasons). Unfortunately, since then the ugly side of the modern day world made its way into the cave, graffiti showed up in the last few years all over what was known as the Warm up Wall but will now have to be called the Graffiti Wall. Because of the smooth paint on the small edges the graffiti has made it nearly impossible to climb some of the harder sit starts that had been done. Hiking graffiti vandals—NOT OK. No worries, the rest of the problems are mostly graffiti-free, steep, quality Bay Area sandstone classics.

Charlie Barrett on Swinger (V5).

About the rock

This is the same Vaqueros Sandstone as the nearby and popular Castle Rock, with good pockets and edges and a really cool (fragile) tufa inside the cave. Steep and hard is what the Stoner Cave is all about with a lot of the problems being short hang and drop-offs because of the 30-foot toprope wall above the cave. Next to the cave is a 60-foot steep slab with a few bolted routes. Uphill to the southeast of the steep slab routes are huge honeycombed tafoni caves that are off limits to climbing but cool to look at.

Number of problems by difficulty

VB	V0	V1	V2	V3	V4	V5	V6	V7	V8	V9	V10	≥V11
0	3	2	4	1	3	3	2	1	0	0	0	0

When to climb

All year can be good with the exception of mid to late winter, which can often be wet in the cave for many days, even weeks after a rain. On the other hand, late fall and early winter (or during light rainstorms any time of year) can sometimes be good in the cave because of the overhanging wall above, which shields the problems from getting wet. Sandstone is brittle, damp sandstone is brittle. Give the rock three to five days to dry after a rain before you climb on it, depending on how much it rained and how sunny and windy that it got after the rain. Summer can sometimes get hot with highs in the 90s and be warned: mosquitoes and a lot of other bugs will be out enjoying themselves as well. Don't fret, spring and fall are packed full of perfect days with fewer bugs, dry stone, and good temps in the 60s and 70s.

Driving Directions

From the North Bay/San Francisco area take US-101 or I-280 to CA-85, then exit Saratoga Ave. and follow it southwest for about a mile to the city of Saratoga. From Saratoga take CA-9/Big Basin Way west into the hills. After about ten miles you will be on top of the hills at the Saratoga Gap intersection with Skyline Blvd. (CA-35), turn right (north) onto Skyline Blvd. (CA-35) and drive about three miles to the parking on the right (east) side of the road at the Grizzly Flat Area of Upper Stevens Creek County Park.

From the South Bay/San Jose area take US-101 or I-280 to CA-85, then exit Saratoga Ave. and follow it southwest for about a mile to the city of Saratoga. From Saratoga take CA-9/Big Basin Way west into the hills. After about ten miles you will be on top of the hills at the Saratoga Gap intersection with Skyline Blvd. (CA-35), turn right (north) onto Skyline Blvd. (CA-35) and drive about three miles to the parking on the right (east) side of the road at the Grizzly Flat Area of Upper Stevens Creek County Park.

From the East Bay/Oakland area take I-680 or I-880 south to San Jose. From I-680 in San Jose take I-280 northwest to CA-17. From I-880 and CA-17 in San Jose follow CA-17 south about four miles to CA-85. Take CA-85 northwest to Saratoga Ave. and follow it southwest for about a mile to the city of Saratoga. From Saratoga take CA-9/Big Basin Way west into the hills. After about ten miles you will be on top of the hills at the Saratoga Gap intersection with Skyline Blvd. (CA-35), turn right (north) onto Skyline Blvd. (CA-35) and drive about three miles to the parking on the right (east) side of the road at the Grizzly Flat Area of Upper Stevens Creek County Park.

From Santa Cruz take River St. northwest out of town—it will turn into CA-9. Follow CA-9 to the top of the hills at the Saratoga Gap intersection with Skyline Blvd. (CA-35), turn left (north) onto Skyline Blvd. (CA-35) and go about three miles to the parking on the right (east) side of the road at the Grizzly Flat Area of Upper Stevens Creek County Park. GPS Parking at Grizzly Flat: 37.290652,-122.154649

Approach

Walk into the park at the trailhead on the opposite side (west side) of Skyline Blvd. from the parking at Grizzly Flat, then head north on the trail along the fence line that parallels Skyline Blvd. After about 0.2 miles take a small trail to the left (west), cross over (the private) Portola Heights Rd. and head downhill into Aquarian Valley. As you enter the forest on the side of the trail you will see a climbing regulation sign. Continue for about another 0.2 miles down the shady canyon to the falls and the cave. To find the Skyline Summit Boulder turn right (north) off the main trail just before (east of) the falls and head up the steep hill toward the Skyline Slabs just below the ridgetop. Total time: 10 to 20 minutes. Total distance: about 0.5 miles. (Skyline Summit Boulder: Time, 15 to 25 minutes; Distance 0.75 miles)

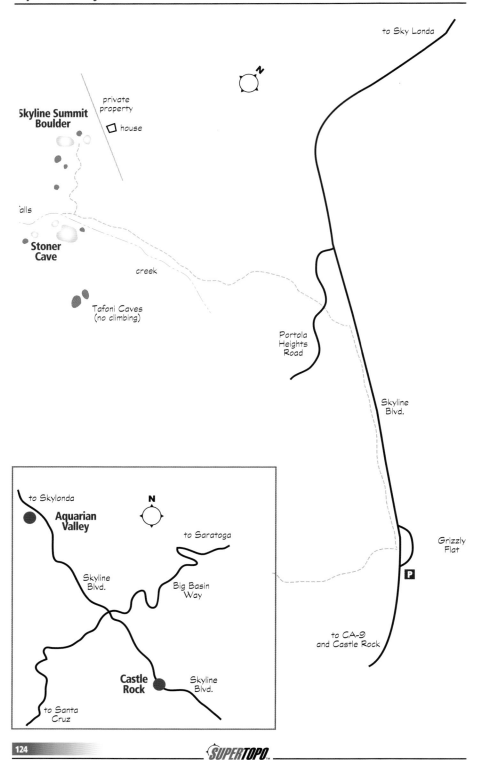

Stoner Cave - Gateway Boulder

On the top of Aquarian Falls the Gateway Boulder forms the right side of the tight corridor entrance to Stoner Cave. GPS Stoner Cave: 37.290033, -122.16675

❏ **1. Gatekeeper V3**★★ Start on the right side of the boulder that marks the entrance to the Stoner Cave on top of the waterfall. Traverse from a good two-hand jug pocket on a mossy overhang above the creek to the left into the tight passageway to the cave and step off at the last good holds before the corner.

❏ **2. Red Eye V6/7**★★ Stand start on good plate like edges and go up into #3 to finish.

❏ **3. Red Tape V4**★★ Start with low left arête and right hand sloper side-pull on overhang. Go up left arête to jug and drop off. Or do the highball V1R/X topout up and right over a bad rocky landing.

Stoner Cave - Graffiti Wall

When I first found the Stoner Cave back at the turn of the century there was only a small amount of stoner graffiti done with charcoal. Now a whole wall has been vandalized with pathetic graffiti.

❏ **4. Sweet Leaf V0**★★ Stand start with jug on top of wall and pull up over onto top. V2 Start mid height on good edges and go up into the stand start. V4 Sit start on small crimpers and do a few moves into the V2.

❏ **5. Graffiti Wall V1**★★ Stand start on high left hand edge and go up left into the V0 stand start of #4.

❏ **6. Graffiti Traverse V2**★★ Stand start on edges on the right side of the wall and move up, then traverse left along the lip into the finish of #5 and #4. The V7/8 sit start is probably harder and unrepeated with the new polished graffiti.

Stoner Cave - Main Face

❏ **7. V2★** Stand or sit start the crack in back of the cave.

❏ **8. The Tufa V2★★** Stand on rock, grab tufas, reach to pocket, mantle Graffiti Wall, step off to Graffiti Wall to finish. Hopefully that's what happens, because falling off this one could be bad even with a pad and spotter for the rocks. And if the big tufa were to break?

❏ **9. Swinger V5★★★** Stand start on sloper scoops down and left of the tufas on #8 with a (don't read the next hint if you don't want beta) toe-hook and bust a big move up to the big tufa on #8, hold the swing, then do #8 to finish.

❏ **10. Rasta V7★★★** Same swinging start as #9 to tufas, then traverse right into #11 to finish.

❏ **11. Aquarius V5★★** Sit start on good left hand two-finger pocket and smaller right hand pocket and make your way up the steep gaston seam to the jug at the lip and drop off.

❏ **12. Aqua Velva V4★★★** Sit start same as #11 on pockets, then traverse up and left into #8 to finish.

❏ **13. Project**

❏ **14. The Stoner Traverse V6★★★** Stand start in big high pocket and traverse right across the steep pockety face, then down a move into the start of #16 and do it to finish. V7 Low start matched on under-cling and do a big move up into the V6 start.

❏ **15. Stoned V5★★** Stand start with good right hand pocket and left hand edge and do a move up into the steep pockety crux of #14 and finish on it.

❏ **16. V1★** Sit start with left hand in lie-back crack/slot and traverse up right to pocket on slab next to bushes and step off.

On the hillside below the Stoner Cave are a few more problems from V0 to V3 and a few short but good toprope/solo highballs and lead climbs.

Skyline Summit Boulder

Just before reaching Aquarian Falls and the left turn across the creek to The Stoner Cave, hang a right up the steep hill from the climbing regulation sign. After stair-climbing up the grassy hill to near the top of the ridge, take a left when the houses (private property) come into view and follow a short trail to the Skyline Summit Boulder, which has a great view from the top of the hill. Just downhill from the boulder are a few bolted routes on the Skyline Slabs.

❏ **17. Skyline Traverse V2★★** Start on the south side of the boulder and traverse uphill around the corner to finish. Thirty feet long, pumpy, and technical.

❏ **18. The Western Traverse V0+★★** Traverse the west face.

❏ **19. V0-V1★** A few problems with big buckets and highball topouts.

❏ **20. Summit or Plummet V4R★★** Steep northwest face on the side of the boulder with a rocky landing. The landing gets especially bad after pulling the crux to the big hueco and dangling over the abyss for the final V0R/X section. **V0R/X Variation:** Start from big hueco.

Le Poseur on Le Stoner Traverse (V6). Photo by Charlie Barrett

Skyline

Problems: **10**

Rock: **Sandstone**

Difficulty: **V0-V6**

A couple all right boulders are north of Castle Rock on Skyline Blvd. They are the same Vaqueros Sandstone and have a few worthy problems each. The first boulder to the north of Castle actually hangs over the east side of Skyline Blvd. The Funny Face Boulder may be a roadside pile but it has a couple fun problems and a scary highball on its steep main face. It also has uncertain access. Don't get too close to the road when doing the Hueco Arête and generally try to be inconspicuous and respectful and it should be all good. The other boulder is actually quite classic, The Alpine Boulder is on the side of the pleasant Alpine Pond with the flat Alpine Pond Trail as a landing. The first ascents were done by longtime locals Dave Caunt and Bruce Morris around the early 1990s.

Alpine Boulder Classics: **Alpine Arête V4** (right arête), **Alpine Face V6** (center of steep face), and V1r (left side of steep face)

Funny Face Boulder Semi-Classics: **Hueco Arête V1r** (over road, be friggin careful.), **Road Rage Traverse V3** and the highball **Truth or Dare V3R** (center of the steep face over bad landing, finish right of tree. Hint: put a pad in tree).

Alpine Boulder Directions/Approach

Alpine Boulder: On the west side of Skyline Blvd. about six miles north of the Saratoga Gap intersection with CA-9 (about nice miles north of Castle Rock) at the

Poser on Alpine Arête (V4) Photo by Sean Brady.

intersection of Skyline and Page Mill Rd. park in the parking lot across Alpine Rd. from Alpine Pond. Cross Alpine Rd. and follow the trail downhill around the west side of the pond for a short five-minute stroll to the boulder on the side of the trail.

Funny Face Boulder Directions/Approach

On Skyline Blvd. 2.0 miles north of the Saratoga Gap intersection with CA-9 (about 4.5 miles north of Castle Rock) park in a dirt turnout on the west side of Skyline Blvd. just before (to the south of) the boulder that is obvious (hopefully not too obvious) hanging over the side of Skyline Blvd. Be careful approaching the boulder.

Farm Hill

Problems: **10**

Rock: **Serpentine**

Difficulty: **V0-V4**

In the rolling hills between I-280 and US-101 near Redwood City are the Farm Hill Boulders and Handley Rock. The main highball face of the Farm Hill Boulder can be seen right off the road and has a couple good arêtes, a fun face and a short, tough traverse. On the hill behind the main face are a couple smaller boulders with a good V0 and a daring V1 over a nasty old mattress. Nearby Handley Rock park is a nice place to check out views of the Bay and do some fun sandstone scrambling, toproping and bouldering.

Classics: **Farm Hill Arête V2** and the direct (no arête) variation **Farm Hill Face V3**, **Farm Hill Traverse V4** (left to right) and the **Right Arête V1**.

Plummet on Farm Hill Traverse (V4).

Driving Directions/Approach

The Farm Hill Boulders are between I-280 and US-101 south of San Francisco and north of San Jose near Redwood City.

From US-101: Take Whipple Ave. exit off US-101 in Redwood City and go west to El Camino Real. Turn left (south) onto El Camino Real and then take a right and head west on Jefferson. As Jefferson begins to climb uphill it will turn into Farm Hill Blvd. Continue uphill (west) on Farm Hill Blvd. and on the right (north) side of the road you will see the boulders.

From I-280: Take Farm Hill Blvd. for about 3⁄4 mile from I-280 east, past Canada College to the boulders which will be visible on the left (north) side of the road.

Handley Rock is off Edgewood Rd. north of Farm Hill. Take Edgewood to Cordilleras then Lakeview to Handley Rock Trail.

Panther Beach

Problems: 10-20

Rock: Sandstone

Difficulty: VB-V?

Panther Beach is sandy and picnicable and at the same time it's also rugged and wild. A nifty stone arch allows for some steep, uninhibited bouldering as well as something cool to look at. Low tide is best unless you want to boulder over the water so check a tide chart before heading out. The sandstone is barely solid enough for climbing and the hand and foot holds are mostly covered in a layer of sand, but the soft, sandy landings and crashing waves give it a fun vibe never the less. A few traverses and hang and drop problems are along the base of the big cliff around the arch. Sharma is said to have bouldered on this wild and exciting beach when he was living nearby. I reckon the good sandy landings combined with the loose sandy holds helped nurture his carefree, go for it style.

The Upper Quarry is inside UC Santa Cruz and climbing (as far as I know) is not allowed. A long traverse and some up problems have been done around the main cliff. A few splitter cracks have also been toproped on the big main cliff. The limestone is sharp and mostly solid except for occasional loose blocks. One of the few, if not the only bouldering fatalities in North America is rumored to have occurred at The Quarry, where I heard that a boulderer dislodged a large block of rock from the traverse wall, causing it to fall off and crush him to death. Be careful not only of loose blocks but of a possible ticket (or worse?) from campus police. Classic: The Limestone Traverse V?

Mike Whipple at Panther Beach.

Driving Directions/Approach

Panther Beach is 6.5 miles north of the last stop light in Santa Cruz on CA-1. Park at the end of a dirt road/turnout on the west (beach) side of the highway and follow a trail downhill toward a cliff with a natural bridge on a big sandy beach.

Big Wave surfing at nearby Mavericks. Photo by Jerry Dodrill.

Granite Creek

Problems: 15

Rock: Granite

Difficulty: VB-V4, mostly VB-V1

Breathtaking views surround these granite crags that are just a short hike from the car. In the heat of summer, when most other inland boulders are sweltering, you can stay cool next to a tide pool and chill out, enjoying some high times after topping out these highball lines. The tide pools here are unique, with crystal clear water, round granite bowling balls, and bright colored starfish and sea anemones. The granite is slick and polished and for anyone who has bouldered on Sierra granite it's also a bit familiar. It can be quite peculiar laybacking a crack that feels like Yosemite and then, krrsplash, a wave crashes nearby, reminding you what a unique place you're hanging out at. Speaking of Yosemite, one of the original pioneers of climbing at Granite Creek, Barry Bates, was also a pioneer in Yosemite with first ascents of classics like Lunatic Fringe and Five + Dime in the early 70s. There is some more bouldering to the north and along the coast to the south all the way into Big Sur. Local climbers have even made up their own rating system for the climbing areas from Carmel to Big Sur. They call it the BS (Big Sur) system. It's like the Yosemite Decimal System; just replace 5 with BS. Of course if you don't like the rating of the climb you're on, then the BS can stand for something else.

Valentine Cullen on The Flake (V0R)

About the rock

Most of the good boulder problems on the main rocks, with the exception of the traverses, are highballs of 15 to 25 feet over rocky landings and require pads, spotters,

mad skills, and big cajones...or a good old-fashioned toprope. If you're thinking about taking the safer approach, there are a few old bolt anchors on top and plenty of cracks for gear. The rock resembles the granite in the Sierra and has a lot of lieback cracks and vertical to slightly overhung, technical faces.

When to climb

Stormy winter days at high tide can be a bit wetter than usual, but it can also be dry anytime of year with the right conditions. Like the areas on the North Coast, it is pretty much a gamble during any season. But unlike a lot of the northern areas, the main rocks at Granite Creek are far enough away from the ocean to avoid getting wet,

Number of problems by difficulty

VB	V0	V1	V2	V3	V4	V5	V6	V7	V8	V9	V10	≥V11
4	5	2	1	1	1	0	0	0	0	0	0	0

usually. Fog sometimes drizzles on the rocks, making them wet and unclimbable. Spring is good and summer is usually perfect with consistent dry conditions and a cool respite from the inland heat waves.

Driving Directions

On CA-1 about eight miles from Rio Rd. (the last major intersection) in south Carmel. Park on the west side of CA-1 in the third pullout south of the Granite Canyon Bridge.

Approach

Hike down a short but steep trail with old wooden stairs precariously attached to the crumbling hillside. The main bouldering wall can be seen facing east (away from the ocean) in a narrow corridor of rock only accessible by down climbing a ten-foot 5.6r. More bouldering can be found below the first pullout south of the bridge. Either hike north along the beach from the main area or park in the first pullout and hike directly downhill on a bad trail with poison oak.

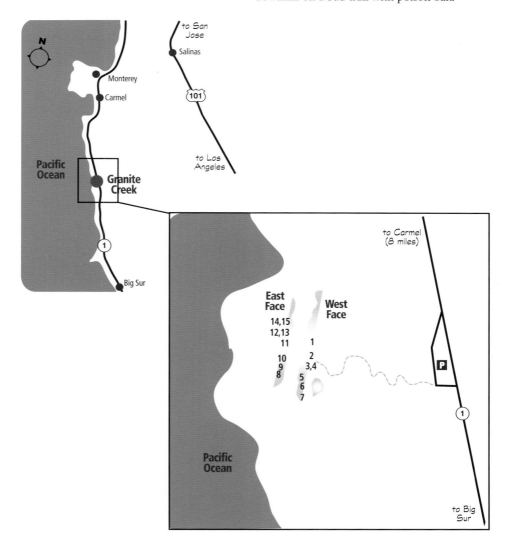

West Face

GPS On top of the West Face opposite the main East Face: 36.4328, -121.9187

☐ **1. 5.4★★** Descent/ascent route.

☐ **2. 5.5★★** Short right hand lieback crack/corner.

☐ **3. V4★★** Sit start on right hand edge and go straight up past small crimpers on short smooth face.

☐ **4. 5.6★★** Corner crack to pink colored topout.

☐ **5. V0★★** Sit start on horizontal crack and go up steep juggy face.

☐ **6. V0★★** Sit or stand start bulgy face.

☐ **7. West Face Traverse V1★★** Start either side traverse the steep juggy face.

East Face

Rocky landing; one large pad or two small pads recommended.

☐ **8. East Face V2R★★★** Stand or sit start on a square cut jug and ascend the slightly overhanging highball face to the left of a vertical brown lieback seam. Bolt(s) on top.

☐ **9. East Face Traverse V1★★** Traverse the base of the wall across the start of #8.

☐ **10.** Toprope?

☐ **11.** 4th Class descent route.

☐ **12. The Corner V0R★★★** Highball left hand lieback corner crack/face.

☐ **13. The Flake V0R★★★** Highball left hand lieback jug flake to the right of an old aid bolt line.

☐ **14. V0R★★★** Highball crack/corner into topout just right of #13.

☐ **15. V3★★** Stand start on under-cling and traverse up and left across the base of the crack wall (#12–#14) to finish on the left either on #12 or further left on #11.

Chris Summit on The East Face (V2R). Photo by Valentine Cullen

Rocklin (Deer Creek Park)

Problems: 50+

Rock: Granite

Difficulty: VB-V8

East of Sacramento, just a few minutes from I-80 on the side of a busy street in the town of Rocklin, is an old granite quarry called Deer Creek Park. It sports about 50 fun and challenging vertical to slightly overhanging problems. A small grove of trees gives shade in the summer and clean flat landings with pieces of carpet straight out of the old school keep the feet dry in between tries. The granite from this quarry was used to build the State Capitol as well as parts of the Central Pacific Railway. About 10-20 good lines from VB to V-hard are concentrated into the main area with more on the surrounding boulders. Bouldering and even a little toprope climbing has been enjoyed here since at least the 1970s. Recently psyched locals like Vic Copeland filled in the gaps, finished off long standing projects and envisioned and climbed some new classics. One of the old school problems that is still classic to this day is the splitter (piton scarred or quarried?) 5.11 finger crack on the far right side of the main wall.

*For more information on Rocklin Bouldering check out Nothern California Bouldering BY SUPERTOPO.

About the rock

Some of the granite is quarried but most all of it seems totally natural. A few of the boulders have the same slopery crimpers that feel like monzonite.

When to climb

All year can be all good with the obvious exceptions of winter when a few of the problems stay wet for days after a rain and the middle of the day in summer when it's often 90-100 degrees.

Kelsey Howard climbs Crack Face (V0).

Driving directions

The town of Rocklin is east of Sacramento on I-80. Exit Rocklin Rd and drive about one mile northwest into downtown Rocklin to Pacific St. Make a left on Pacific St and go about a half a mile to the boulders in the small Deer Creek Park on the right (northwest) side of the road just before (north of) Farron St. There is no parking on Pacific but parking on Farron is possible. The only other close parking would be in the businesses nearby, but make sure to ask for permission. Heres a few of the classics;

Pacific Street Wall:
Pacific Street Traverse V0-V5★★ High - low.
Quarry Pinch V8★★★ Far left face on P.S.W.
Right Leaning Crack V3★★★ Right of Q.P.
Crack Face V0 or V4★★★ Center V0 right V4.
Pinscar Crack V2 or V3★★★ P.S. Wall right.
The Bayou - aka The Pit:
Slab Crack VBX★★★ Highball splitter in Pit.
The Dihedral V0X★★★ Highball corner in Pit.
The Loaf V0 or V1★★★ Mantel V0 - Arete V1.
Children of the Night V2★★★ Blunt arete.
Deer Creek Slab V5★★★ Center slab patina.

The Bar

Problems: **50+**

Rock: **Greenstone and Schist**

Difficulty: **VB-V7**

In the Sierra foothills next to the Middle Fork of the American River near the town of Auburn is a collection of sculpted, water-polished boulders and cliffs known as The Bar. Located inside the Auburn State Recreation Area at the Mammoth Bar OHV Park, bouldering is considered a legitimate activity. The river is close to a lot of the boulders so the higher water levels of winter and spring can submerge some of the problems. Fall is usually perfect, with cool temps and dry problems. In summer the river will be lower and most of the boulders dry but it can get hot. No worries, just downstream (make sure its downstream) from the Murderers Bar Rapid are some good swimming holes that are no farther than a stumble from most of the boulders.

*For more information on The Bar Bouldering check out Nothern California Bouldering BY SUPERTOPO.

About the rock

A mix of green river stone, schist and water polished volcanic.

When to climb

All year. Summer is hot but you can swim in the river and climb in the shade. Winter and spring are wet and a lot of the problems get submerged in the higher river but there is still a lot dry stone along the hillsides.

Driving directions

From I-80 in Auburn take the Foresthill exit and go about 2.5 miles east to Old Foresthill Rd (passing over the highest bridge in California!) Turn right on Old Foresthill Rd and go about 1.5 miles to the park entrance on the left.

Approach

Park in the main parking lot at the bottom of the dirt road and hike along the river

Sean Brady on Handlebar (V3).

downstream to the obvious large cliff and boulders. Or park in a large turnout on the right side of the road about 3/4 of the way down and hike directly to the top of the big cliff and then down to the boulders. This way is recommended: it's steeper but has less "Bar Hopping." Heres a few of the classics;

Bar Rocks:
The Bar Traverse V3★★★ Traverse Bar Rock.
The Crawl V4★★ Traverse up left over rock.
Lucky Ace V5★★★★ Graffitti river boulder.
Handlebar Boulder:
V7★★ Sit start down left of Handlebar.
Handlebar V3★★★★ Sit start on handlebar jug (V3) or edges below (V4) or direct V5
Handlebar Dyno V4★★★ Dyno up right!
Handlebar Traverse V5★★ Gaston-Handlebar
Flowmaster V6★★ Start Handlebar traverse lip right to end on Gaston Problem. **V7 Var:** Do Handlebar Dyno into Flowmaster.
Gaston Problem V6★★★★ Start on face right of the Handlebar and go up gastons - V7 sit.
Roof Rock:
The Roof V4★★ Sit start exit right drop off.
The Face V7★★ Same sit up left face to jug.

MORE FROM SUPERTOPO

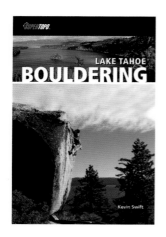

Lake Tahoe Bouldering

$29.95 Available at www.supertopo.com

Lake Tahoe is quickly becoming California's largest summer bouldering area. There are more than 35 areas with more than 1,400 problems and new challenges are discovered every week. What sets Tahoe apart is not just the numbers, it is the variety. You can climb Joshua Tree style rock by the lake or climb Yosemite-esque holds in the forest or drive 30 minutes east to the desert and climb impeccable volcanic pockets. It is all here, it is all year round, and even this book, offering the most complete coverage yet on the subject, can only whet your appetite.

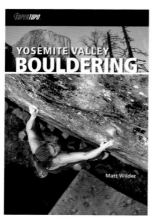

YOSEMITE VALLEY BOULDERING

$27.95 Available at www.supertopo.com

Yosemite Valley is one of the best granite bouldering areas in the world. This guide aims to inspire current and future Yosemite boulderers and makes Valley bouldering more accessible through clear descriptions, detailed topos, and numerous photos. This book includes many new problems and even completely new areas. From Camp 4 holdless desperates to classic moderates in serene settings, you will find the problems to suit your mood and motivation.

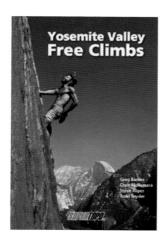

YOSEMITE VALLEY FREE CLIMBS

$29.95 Available at www.supertopo.com

This guidebook includes over 230 of the best routes in Yosemite Valley, from 16-pitch trad climbs to one-pitch sport routes. While many hard Yosemite test-pieces are included, this book focuses on topropes, crags, and multi-pitch climbs in the 5.4-5.9 range. We also include formerly obscure climbs to provide more options for avoiding crowds. As in all SuperTopo books, the authors personally climbed and documented each route with meticulous care to create the most detailed and accurate topos ever published.

MORE FROM SUPERTOPO

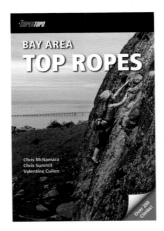

BAY AREA TOP ROPES

Price: $19.95 Available at www.supertopo.com

Bay Area Top Ropes includes over 260 climbs within a 2 hour drive of San Francisco. Included are over 19 areas from North Coast, South Bay, East Bay, San Francisco and Sierra Foothills. All the classic spots are in this book: Castle Rock, Mt. Tam, Split Rock, Mt. Diablo as well as a number of lesser known spots on the North Coast. In addition, this book includes a 20 pages of information that help the transition from the gym to outdoors. Author Chris Summit personally climbed and mapped almost every route to ensure the accuracy of the information.

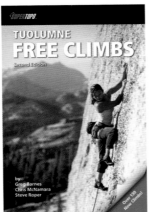

TUOLUMNE FREE CLIMBS - 2nd Edition

Price: $26.95 Available at www.supertopo.com

Tuolumne Free Climbs includes over 240 of the best routes in Tuolumne Meadows, from 14-pitch trad climbs to one-pitch sport routes. This book focuses on top ropes, crags, and multi-pitch climbs in the 5.4-5.9 range. Includes formerly obscure climbs to provide more options for avoiding crowds. As in all SuperTopo books, the authors personally climbed and documented each climb with meticulous care to create the most detailed and accurate topos ever published.

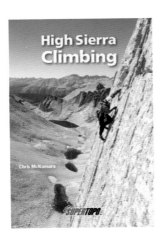

HIGH SIERRA CLIMBING

$24.95 Available at www.supertopo.com

This guidebook includes 26 of the best High Sierra alpine climbs, ranging in difficulty from 3rd class to 5.11c. Most of these climbs are well-protected, 10 to 15 pitches long, and ascend some of the best alpine granite anywhere. Whether you plan to scramble up the 3rd class East Ridge of Mt. Russell, climb the 5.7 East Face of Mt. Whitney, or ascend the epic 18-pitch Sun Ribbon Arête, our guidebook will ensure you spend minimum time getting off-route and maximum time enjoying the climbing.

About the Author

Chris Summit was born to climb. A
Northern California native he started
climbing and bouldering at his local North
Bay crags Sunset Rocks and Mt St Helena
20 years ago and since has authored a total
of 7 climbing guidebooks on climbing and
bouldering in the area. He self published
his first guidebook, the local and now
out of print Wine Country Rocks and
for Supertopo Bay Area Bouldering,
Northern California Bouldering, Tuolumne
Bouldering and the brand new Bay Area
Top Ropes. He also authored, with Tom
Slater and Maximus Press, the bible of all
rock climbing in Nor Cal; California Road-
trip Northern California. Currently he is
working on a new guidebook for the Bay
Area by Supertopo with all styles of rock
climbing from sport and trad climbing
to top roping and bouldering. Chris has
bouldered V10 and sport climbed 5.13 but
his specialty is finding and climbing new
rocks in uncharted areas. He also loves
teaching climbers of all ages and skill levels
about the benefits of indoor climbing and
the priceless rewards of climbing in the
great outdoors.

Photo by Jim Thornburg

Index

CLIMBERS, the **ENVIRONMENT** and **ACCESS**
are all interconnected
Know how you fit in. ››

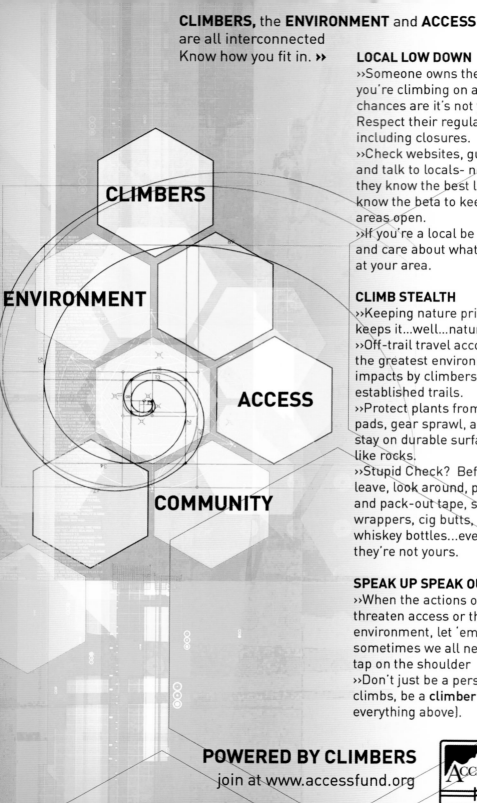

CLIMBERS

ENVIRONMENT

ACCESS

COMMUNITY

LOCAL LOW DOWN
››Someone owns the land that you're climbing on and chances are it's not you. Respect their regulations, including closures.
››Check websites, guidebooks, and talk to locals- not only do they know the best lines, they know the beta to keep the areas open.
››If you're a local be informed and care about what happens at your area.

CLIMB STEALTH
››Keeping nature pristine keeps it...well...natural.
››Off-trail travel accounts for the greatest environmental impacts by climbers - stay on established trails.
››Protect plants from packs, pads, gear sprawl, and feet; stay on durable surfaces - uh, like rocks.
››Stupid Check? Before you leave, look around, pick-up and pack-out tape, spilt chalk, wrappers, cig butts, whiskey bottles...even if they're not yours.

SPEAK UP SPEAK OUT
››When the actions of others threaten access or the environment, let 'em know- sometimes we all need a little tap on the shoulder
››Don't just be a person who climbs, be a **climber** (psst...see everything above).

POWERED BY CLIMBERS
join at www.accessfund.org

ACCESS FUND

your climbing future